D1624189

Douglas McGregor, Revisited

Douglas McGregor, Revisited

Managing THE Human Side OF THE Enterprise

GARY HEIL
WARREN BENNIS
DEBORAH C. STEPHENS

John Wiley & Sons, Inc.

New York • Chichester • Weinheim • Brisbane • Singapore • Toronto

*This book is dedicated to
all those who incarnate
McGregor's thinking and ideals.*

ISBN 0-471-31462-5

10 9 8 7 6 5 4 3 2 1

Contents

Contents

Preface

Simple truths are the hardest to come to—and the most powerful to use. Douglas McGregor knew how to find the simple, powerful truths about the changing nature of work, and of man's place in the workplace. These ideas lie at the heart of this book.

This book doesn't claim to introduce radical new ideas to the world of management. To do so would fly in the face of the essence of Douglas McGregor's ideas. Rather, we are introducing the work of this important thinker and leader because we believe that McGregor's ideas are more important and relevant than ever before. The question is not whether his ideas are better today than ever before, but whether the world of work is ready to be affected by his thinking. We welcome the debate that this book should kick off. The questions he raised deal with the key matters facing all managers in today's economy.

Douglas McGregor's significance was in applying a better understanding of how people behave in the business world. As he asked in the title of an address he delivered in 1962, "Why not exploit behavioral science?" He was the first to apply behavioral science findings to the world of business. Naturally such an approach didn't lend itself to easy answers. To promise easy solutions to human problems would be disingenuous at best. His simple writing explored the implications of how to manage differently given what we have learned about human behavior.

Douglas McGregor believed that as the world became more complex and as technology enabled companies to be more competitive, the dynamics of the people in an organization would become more important to the success of these groups. He believed fundamentally in what he called "the Human Side of Enterprise;" and he believed that we were not close to optimizing the effectiveness of organized human effort. In fact, he was frustrated by the way we approached organizational improvement. We were asking the wrong questions in the wrong places. In his essay "The Manager, Human Nature, and Human Sciences," he wrote, "Strictly speaking, the answer to the question managers so often ask of behavioral scientists—'How do you motivate people?'—is, 'You don't.' Man is by nature motivated." In fact, he believed that we first needed to think about the problem differently before we had any chance of solving it.

That meant behaving as individuals in a manner that was consistent with what we know to be true about human behavior. It meant treating people as individuals, each with his or her own set of values and motivations. Corporations could be seen not as machines with interchangeable human parts, but as living organizations that could be designed to enable its people to grow and learn while achieving a mutual business goal. McGregor recognized the importance of caring about people's attitudes, which dictated behavior. He pointed out that we are defined by how we think, and that if we don't change our basic assumptions about people, we will never change what we do.

So why didn't his ideas take root? Quite simply, because the world would have had to change too radically. As we point out in Chapter 2, today the new economy accommodates McGregor's ideas in a far more dynamic manner than any past form of industrial organization. The rise of the networked economy, the growing power of front-line workers, the shift in power from mass producer to individual consumer, and the increased capacity of the workplace to offer meaningful enterprise; all these conditions lend hope to a world of work that we could call "McGregorian."

We hope this book will start a conversation about why we take actions that are often so inconsistent with what we know about people. The questions are key: Do reward systems work? Are people inherently motivated or not? Are organizations living things or not? McGregor taught us that there are no right or wrong answers to these questions. Yet the act of asking these questions, and of trying to learn the answers by ourselves, creates meaning.

In essence, we all are *McGregorian,* and we hope that this book helps expose others to these ideas, and helps keep a healthy debate alive.

GARY HEIL
WARREN BENNIS
DEBORAH C. STEPHENS

Acknowledgments

This space is simply too short to thank all of the people who have supported this project. We would, however, like to give our deepest thanks to those who have traveled this road long before we set out on our first journey. Douglas McGregor, Abraham Maslow, Chris Argyris, Carl Frost, and Joseph Scanlon are just a few of the people to whom we owe a debt of gratitude. They have provided context from which we have tried to learn.

The authors are truly thankful for the continued support of Pat Colvard, who always believed in the importance of this project. We also thank the Wiley team, in particular Jeanne Glasser. This project was not an easy one and Jeanne was the glue that held it together. Finally, we thank Tom Ehrenfeld for his contributions.

G.H.
W.B.
D.C.S.

Part 1

Why McGregor Matters

1

Why McGregor Matters

The world that Douglas McGregor spoke of is here. In today's interconnected economy of bits and bytes, of wired companies and real-time business, the spread of technology has made the human side of enterprise more important than ever. When companies can knock each other off with greater ease and speed as their technological edge becomes ever more replicable, then their enduring source of competitive advantage will be found not in goods and services, but in their collective brain power. Those businesses that thrive today are not necessarily those with the most valuable resources, the greatest market share, or the most capital (though none of these hurt); rather, those businesses that are able to tap their human potential in the most productive manner are the ones who enjoy enduring success.

This is the world that Douglas McGregor envisioned.

I will venture the prediction that we will succeed in increasing our utilization of the human potential in organizational settings only as we succeed in creating conditions that generate a meaningful way of life. . . . [Joseph] Scanlon's lasting contribution is his recognition—now effectively demonstrated in action—that one cannot successfully tackle this

3

central task of management with gimmicks or procedures or programs. The real task of management is to create conditions that result in genuine collaboration throughout the organization. To create such conditions is to create a way of life. This is the central conclusion to which the findings of social science are pointing today. ("The Scanlon Plan: Through a Psychologist's Eyes," *Leadership and Motivator*, MIT Press, 1966, pp. 140–141)

Douglas McGregor would love to have lived today, for the old saying that necessity is the mother of invention rings true. All of his passion for creating a more human organization would have been, as he predicted, more necessary and, therefore, more achievable. In his day, managers could ignore his fundamental message. Paying attention to the human side of management simply wasn't a primary requirement for success in his day. Large, bureaucratic organizations that mass produced goods could treat their countless workers as interchangeable parts in a mechanistic system.

Today, however, McGregor cannot be ignored. Our age of technological dazzle has led to a paradox: the networked economy and ubiquity of computers have given companies a more natural quality than ever before. They are no longer built as impersonal machines with predictable results, but emerge as living, unpredictable entities with organic qualities. And as such, companies are finding that their enduring source of competitive advantage rests within their human capital. In his work, McGregor anticipated such a shift in working conditions—not necessarily because he was so technologically prescient, but because he recognized that as the world became more complex, the importance of releasing human potential at every level of the organization would emerge as the most appropriate working model.

McGregor stressed the fundamental importance of dealing with the human side of enterprise. Managers had to see their employees not as cogs in the machine, but as living beings with individual goals. This was not, in his view, a limitation, but a condition that opened up countless opportunities. When organized properly, groups of people working together could realize their aspirations in a far more powerful and deep-rooted manner than they could have imagined. Those leaders who saw these opportunities and made the bold organizational choice to realize their potential, both individually and collectively, would leapfrog anyone with a more traditional mindset.

Since McGregor laid out his vision of this humanistic workplace more than three decades ago, his message has become far more resonant. The nature of work today makes McGregor's theories more relevant and necessary than ever. The technology that he anticipated has changed the landscape in ways that make the human element even more important than he probably had dreamed. In fact, the enormous spread of technology into every facet of business life has had the ironic impact of making the humans who run these tools more critical than ever. Consider the changes in business today that are discussed next.

Personalization

Today virtually everything that a company delivers to a customer is unique. What were once commodities have become discrete items produced for individuals—at the scale of mass markets. Levi Strauss, for example, now offers personalized jeans to its customers. Individuals can walk into designated stores, get measured by employees, and have the company produce a pair of jeans that meets their individual body shape. Dell Computer, one of the best-performing companies of the past decade, attributes much of its ability to outpace its opponents to its radically different business model. Unlike most computer operators that mass produce huge batches of machines that are then sold by retailers, Dell grew by taking individual orders for computers over the phone, and eventually over the Internet. Factory workers then created the individual machines, which were shipped directly to consumers. This personalized approach gave the company a huge advantage in its inventory turn and resultant cost of capital, and built customer loyalty through the individual's sense of ownership of their PC. In each instance, these companies have used existing technology to produce a unique, personalized product experience for each customer.

Yet computers, which can personalize products, cannot humanize them. For that you need humans. With every transaction, people become more important in the process. That's because the ability to customize a product to the individual makes the *relationship* with the customer the key transaction. Gathering information, and above all developing trust, have become the key source of sustainable competitive advantage. The smartest companies today recognize this process and leverage the human relationships that are fostered by new technology. In their books and speeches, authors/consultants Donald Peppers and Martha Rodgers describe a "One-to-One" world in which companies grow not by selling their goods to a larger audience, but by learning how to sell more products and services to existing customers. This simple turn of business thinking is predicated by companies' increasing ability to compile sophisticated information on what their customers need, and then respond nimbly to this data. Hotels can tap into the client database, for example, to find new services to sell them, just as other service companies can brainstorm new products to add to their mix. Loyal customers to web sites such as Amazon.com now receive customized recommendations for books and CDs based on their personal buying history. Again, the human relationship serves as the platform upon which these companies deliver greater value.

Power Shifts to Customers

The power is shifting in commercial relationships as customers continue to be taught that they can have it their way. Not only are the best companies using the web and other technologies to have continuous, anytime, anyplace dialogues with their customers, but a growing number of companies have embraced the idea that choice is value.

Once upon a time, producers set the rules of the game. Ma Bell let customers choose what color phone they wanted—as long as it was black. Car manufacturers introduced this year's model to eager masses of aficionados. And hotels, airlines, or other large service providers dictated the prices it would offer to customers. Today all these offerings are up for grabs. The breakup of AT&T is a sign of the explosion of choices available to consumers today. Amidst the cornucopia of portable, personalized, stylized, and miniaturized products, a simple black phone's value today rests solely in its status as a retro collectible. Consumers can also choose from not only thousands of phone lines, but perhaps millions of variations of service from countless carriers. Moreover, automobiles are now cranked out in smaller, more customized batches to worldwide consumers. And in the area of prices, consumers today are turning to web auctions to find, and often set, the lowest conceivable prices for services that were once non-negotiable.

Again, such changes place ever greater importance on the *people* of an organization. As goods and services become ever more commoditized, then the human experience backing them rises in value—and the consequences of failing to deliver a satisfying transaction escalate. Consider the explosion of "spite sites," web sites detailing the poor service people have received from individual corporations. When a recent customer was unhappy with his experience at Starbucks, he undertook what became a nationally-known campaign of complaint against the company. Other dissatisfied customers have created web sites and campaigns against companies like USAir or Apple. Virtually every large company today, in fact, finds itself targeted by once-loyal customers who turn critics when they receive poor human response. These customers are not angry with the products—but with the lackluster human experience they have come to expect.

The Internet Economy

In today's Internet world, personalization matters more than ever. Web companies today are finding that they are competing on the unique experience that their digital presence delivers. Companies that provide an environment for people to share their passion enjoy returns beyond any reasonable expectation. In fact, they find that because experience can be digitized and thus easily replicated, the ability to produce relationships fuels its own success. e-Bay CEO Meg Whitman attributes her company's success to a "network effect" in which the quantity and caliber of the conversation taking place on the company's boards becomes a lure to more consumers. The sheer human inter-action that e-Bay hosts becomes a self-reinforcing foundation of its success. Providing a replicable site for human energy has become a source of competitive advantage.

Service: The Only Enduring Brand

As the distinction between products and services becomes a blurry, al-most nonexistent line, the importance of loyalty becomes ever more im-portant. People rarely get emotional about software—but they do about a company's prowess at solving their problems. The ability of companies to support their employees as they maintain human relationships with customers becomes the core value for growth. In everything from e-mail service to other goodies, web merchants who recognize the value of per-sonal data are giving away physical goods to customers who will share their personal information. They recognize that the blurring of products and services makes the underlying human transaction ever more critical.

Customers increasingly look to companies as trusted sources of au-thority that will help them make the right choices. When children, for example, begin to derive as much pleasure from designing their doll as playing with it, that places an increased premium on the ability of the people in that doll-maker's company to provide a welcoming experi-ence for making those choices.

Innovation: The Only Way to Maintain Margins

In today's economy, technological prowess is mere table stakes. At a time when any significant technological lead can be quickly repro-duced, the race is won by those companies that are willing and able to constantly reinvent what they produce. Look at how Amazon.com has adopted the auction format of e-Bay. As the first company to conduct consumer auctions for collectibles on a grand scale, e-Bay became one of the fastest growing and popular web sites ever. As noted above, it leveraged its popularity into higher visibility, which in turn helped its stock price and drew greater crowds to the site. And yet, it still found itself with a new competitor: Amazon.com, which launched its own auction feature, becoming an instant player that could give e-Bay a run for the money. Amazon was able to leverage its community of on-line buyers into a viable competitor to e-Bay soon after the launch of the auction feature.

Yet machines don't innovate—people do. It takes an inspired and committed workforce to produce innovative products. How could Apple Computer revive itself from a near-death bed? By introducing a line of better designed computers—the iMac—that captured enormous market share. In so doing, the company changed consumer's relationship to their computers—turning them once more from commodity boxes to unique expressions of taste—while lifting the company's fortune and stock price. CEO Steve Jobs, the man behind the company's turnaround, recognizes the critical need for a corporate culture that enables such personalized technology. These products do not come from compliance, but from a culture where people have passion to express themselves.

Organizational Life

Organizational life has become far more complex, organic, and unpredictable than before. Today's organization bears little resemblance to the top-down, bureaucratic, hide-bound, rule-driven hierarchy that emerged during the first two-thirds of this century. The largest and most significant companies today grow and shrink in the time it used to take automakers to produce a new line of cars. Scores of independent contractors function as free agents who skip from company to company rather than work for one organization for life.

These virtual, shifting organizations are bound more by trust than authority. In his book, *Trust,* writer Francis Fukymaya argues that trust functions as a form of social glue binding people and organizations together. He recognizes that the digitized world amplifies the importance of trust as a vital resource among groups of people in common enterprise. As greater numbers of employees work in far-flung locations, and companies devolve into virtual networks of suppliers and independent contractors, the evanescent glue of human trust becomes ever more important as a business imperative. Trust differs radically from authority, which McGregor found a shaky source of power in any organization:

> Some of our most troublesome problems in managing the human resources of industry in the United States today are directly traceable to the assumption that authority is an absolute and to inappropriate attempts to control behavior which flow from this assumption. (*The Human Side of Enterprise*, p. 21)

In the same piece of writing, McGregor elaborated on authority's flaws in an increasingly decentralized world.

> Authority, as a means of influence, is certainly not useless, but for many purposes it is less appropriate than persuasion or professional help. Exclusive reliance upon authority encourages countermeasures, minimal performance, even open rebellion. The dependence—as in the case of adolescent in the family—is simply not great enough to guarantee compliance. (*The Human Side of Enterprise*, p. 26)

Technology Has Surpassed Our Humanity

Wired magazine editor Kevin Kelly says we have seen all the changes that technology will create, and that our biggest challenge will be catching up with the people side. In other words, we've gotten better at everything technological but have made less substantial strides in the people arena. Individuals now have the ability to conduct global research from their desktop. Cutting edge financial companies have the ability to slice and dice databases of consumer information to simultaneously offer millions of different individuals credit cards that are customized to their needs and credit profiles. Affinity groups around passions and vocations can form instant networks over the web. And yet, few people have figured out how to manage the real human changes that these technologies bring about.

And that's where Douglas McGregor comes in.

Managing the Human Side of Enterprise

McGregor was above all a futurist. He foresaw the end of a mechanist view of management long before people were ready to hear such a viewpoint. Prior to his thinking, the prevailing view toward organizations was one of a machine: driven from the top, ruled by authority, predictable outcomes from fixed inputs, and staffed with interchangeable people.

McGregor challenged managers to think of human organizations more as a biologist than a mechanic. As he wrote in his book, *The Human Side of Enterprise,*

> Managerial practice appears to reflect at least a tacit belief that motivating people *to work* is a "mechanical" problem. There are certain similarities between this view of man at work and Newton's Laws of Motion. To a considerable degree, man has been perceived to be like a physical body at rest. It requires the application of external forces to set him in motion—to motivate him to work. Consequently, extrinsic rewards and punishments are the obvious and appropriate "forces" to be utilized in controlling organized human effort.

He believed that such machine metaphors inhibited us from finding a better and simpler way of building more effective organizations. In that same essay, he continued:

> He is an "organic" system, not a mechanical one. Inputs of energy (sun, food, water, etc.) are transformed by him into outputs of behavior (including intellectual activities and emotional responses, as well as observable actions). His behavior is influenced by relationships between his characteristics as an organic system (I) and the environment (E). Creating these relationships is a matter of *releasing* his energy in certain ways rather than others. We do not motivate him, because he *is* motivated. When he is not, he is dead. This is the sense in which the behavioral

scientist distinguishes between an organic and a purely mechanical theory of human nature.

McGregor's belief in the manager as a gardener, or system architect, allowed people to take a radically different approach to work. Leading self-organizing systems enabled people to cultivate rather than direct change; to enable people to realize their potential rather than "fix" them. People are living organisms and communities of work are capable of renewal, adaptation, and change, and can't be fixed. McGregor recognized that real change happens only when a community of interest decides it wants to be different and the obstacles to renewal are removed.

He believed that as in any organic system, the more that you broke the system into its subparts the more complicated the system became. As we have learned in science, rarely are cause and effect apparent in a complicated system. Overly simplified models that attempt to give easy answers to complex problems just distract us and delay real, meaningful efforts to identify a better path.

He thought that every management interaction was a complex challenge that involved a wide array of factors, such as the personal variables of the leader/manager (attitudes, assumptions about what works, habits, beliefs, values, experiences, prejudices, etc.), the characteristics of the followers (habits, beliefs, experiences, education, values, prejudices, self-confidence, etc.) and the political/social milieu in which people work (work structure, policies, economic environment, geographic location, espoused values of the organization, perceived mission, etc.). "Perhaps the most general statement of the potential contribution that behavioral science can make to management would be this: Our present knowledge indicates that there are a number of important characteristics of individuals *and* of the work environment that conventional management practice does not take into account. The variables that most managers do not take into account are necessary, but they are not sufficient to explain organized human effort. Since these additional variables are not recognized, the relationships among them are unknown to these managers. Existing behavioral science knowledge affords the possibility of improved control of organized human effort through the inclusion of these variables and their interrelationships in managerial practice."

He embraced the complexity that was management and resisted any attempt to distill one-size-fits-all solutions to complex problems. He resisted attempts to prescribe believing that every interaction was as unique as the people involved.

McGregor's perspective anticipated the "systems thinking" approach that predominates a great deal of managerial theory today. This school of thought posits that myriad forces within large systems are interrelated, and that one can begin to see how their forms of behavior emerge when viewed as a whole. "Behavior of a system is a consequence of interaction of its parts, parts that themselves must be understood and interconnected," wrote pioneer Jay Forrester in "System Dynamics." As McGregor noted in his book, *The Human Side of Enterprise:*

> The outstanding fact about relationships in the modern industrial organization is that they involve a high degree of interdependence. Not only are subordinates dependent upon those above them in the organization for satisfying their needs and achieving their goals, but managers at every level are dependent upon all those below them for achieving both their own and organizational goals. (p. 23)

The implications of such a system's view are critical. McGregor was continually asked the inevitable question that we have all been asked. "I agree with your theory and I am committed to making it happen, but how do you make it happen?" His commitment to learning our way into the future was evident in all of his work, and this probably accounted for much of the resistance he encountered to his ideas. In his day, as today, people sought easy solutions to what proved to be stubborn and intractable challenges. Although there were no answers, he believed that we were dealing with a science in which certain laws about people did apply (just as in science). He strongly felt that much of what passed for good management in his day was antithetical to what was known about human nature in organizations and that most of our attempts to improve were doomed because it failed to see people as people. It seemed to make the assumption that they were in fact more like resources.

He wanted his students to learn as much as they could about the research that had been done in the behavioral sciences because he believed that only by understanding these findings could we conduct more efficient experiments. For without using existing research in our learning design, we were more likely to conduct experiments that led us to more of what we did yesterday or to try and reinvent the wheel; that is, spend time learning what others had already found.

McGregor wanted us to embrace complexity without being paralyzed by it. He wanted us to conduct simple experiments in a complex system. He wanted managers to include all people in the organization in the planning and execution of those experiments. Even though he tried to hide his biases, many were not well disguised.

His belief in the real power of participation was obvious. He believed that it was important not because it was tactical, but because it was the way the world worked. People simply did not work hard at things they did not have a hand in creating. Rather, they worked hard to achieve deeply felt needs of theirs. His philosophy was greatly informed by Maslow's hierarchy of needs. As McGregor wrote,

> All human behavior is directed toward the satisfaction of needs. From birth to death, the individual is engaged in a constant attempt to satisfy his varied, complex, and sometimes conflicting needs. Any given behavior is a resolution of forces arising in part within him and in part in the environmental situation. (*Leadership and Motivation*, p. 154)

In this respect, McGregor believed that most managers used authority to effect behavioral change through threat or reward, both of which he saw as limiting the employee's ability to realize their needs. He believed that managers could also use their control in a positive manner—to augment their employees natural desire to satisfy their needs rather than rig it.

His belief that we must deal with whole persons if we hope to gain their commitment was also apparent. The idea that people could hide their emotions or leave them at home were ludicrous. As he noted, we really wanted emotions at work but we wanted only the ones that we wanted—loyalty, commitment, and so on.

McGregor saw behavior modification models that used what he called "gimmicks" as doomed to fail. McGregor wanted to see behavior as intrinsically motivated. McGregor railed against any form of control that stifled the innate drive of the individual worker. Sometimes these forms of control would be what he called gimmicks, managerial tricks to gain some form of compliance by individuals. Other times the gimmick would simply be the exertion of authority. Regardless of the form the gimmick took, he decried external attempts to coerce behavior as doomed, short-term measures.

One of McGregor's most important contributions to management today underlies all of these movements. He asked every manager to view management not merely as a toolbox of tasks but as an integrative function that asks them to examine their deepest held beliefs about people and the nature of work. In the next chapter, we will look more closely at this fundamental challenge.

The McGregor Legacy

While Douglas McGregor spoke often about the need for managers to examine their operating theories, his ultimate goal was for these theories to manifest themselves as new working models. Today his ideas have become the governing theories behind several important managerial tools and tactics. His beliefs inform many of the practices of today's leading companies—everything from greater decentralization to virtual organizations to competing by design—embody the best of this thinking. McGregor's most influential legacy may be *open book management* (OBM), which hundreds of companies now practice as a form of employee involvement and continuous improvement.

Open book management evolved out of the Scanlon Plan, a form of management that recognized the value of joint labor-management participation by devising a model plantwide bonus system that focused on reducing costs, improving productivity, and eliminating waste. The practice was developed by Joseph Scanlon, a steelworker and union leader during the depression who became a lecturer at MIT in the 1940s. His plan was based on the dignity and untapped potential of every human being.

Scanlon expressed the basic philosophy of his plan:

> What we are actually trying to say is simply this: That the average worker knows his own job better than anyone else, and that there are a great many things that he could do if he has a complete understanding of the necessary. Given this opportunity of expressing his intelligence and ingenuity, he becomes a more useful and valuable citizen in any given community or in any industrial operation.

McGregor, who knew and worked with Scanlon at MIT, endorsed his plan wholeheartedly, saying, "I need only mention the Scanlon Plan as the outstanding embodiment of [participation and consultative management] in practice." He saw in this system

The McGregor Legacy *(Continued)*

a method for aligning the interests of workers and their organization. As he wrote, "The Scanlon Plan is not a formula, a program, or a set of procedures. It is a way of industrial life—a philosophy of management—which rests on theoretical assumptions entirely consistent with Theory Y." Unfortunately this plan failed to be adopted widespread. "Few managements wished to involve the workers to the degree contemplated in the plan or were willing to make the sustained efforts to maintain the plan over time" (Derber, *The American Idea of Industrial Democracy,* p. 479.) Today several major companies, such as Lincoln Electric and Herman Miller carry on the tradition.

Out of the grounding of the Scanlon Plan has arisen a more popular managerial practice: open book management, a system of sharing financial information with employees of business units. This plan was made famous by the Springfield Remanufacturing Corporation (SRC). Formerly a division of International Harvester, this unit was purchased in a leveraged buyout by CEO Jack Stack and other managers. Faced with a huge debt load, Stack decided that the best way to turn around operations was to share financial data with every employee in the company, and expect them to put this information to good use. The company began to regularly share financial data with the employees in small groups, and asked them to play what he called "The great game of business," in which people were expected to take individual responsibility for improving the numbers. The approach paid off: SRC is now a $100 million company with a healthy core business. Moreover, it has become so adept at the managerial practice it innovated that the company serves as a model for others who want to learn open book management. The company markets OBM instructional material through a teaching subsidiary.

(continued)

The McGregor Legacy *(Continued)*

OBM is now practiced by thousands of companies as a means of involving their employees in meaningful work. OBM asks its employees to take a system approach to their work by understanding exactly how the company makes money—how the work they do translates into specific financial consequences at both an individual and overall level. This approach asks individuals to take ownership of their own actions, and it pays accordingly: Many companies give their OBM employees sweat equity in the business, and expect them to enhance its value through their participation. Journalist John Case says of open book management, "In open-book companies, people learn to follow the numbers and help make decisions. They learn to think and act like owners, like businesspeople, and not like hired hands." Douglas McGregor would certainly endorse that.

Finally, there is one other significant change in managerial practice that would thrill Douglas McGregor—the growth of distributed Human Resources (HR). In his essay, "The Staff Function in Human Relations," McGregor anticipated one of the most significant changes to human resources management in the past several years: the erosion of this function as a discrete department with authority over all others. Today, many companies such as Xerox and Peoplesoft are beginning to implement a form of "distributed" HR in which employees tap into centralized databases to exert more personal control over the administration of their benefits. This type of practice facilitates greater responsibility of leaders at smaller units to handle the human needs of their unit. Books such as *The Leadership Engine: How Winning Companies Build Leaders at Every Level,* by Noel Tichy, for example, show how smart companies create internal conditions that enable individuals to develop leadership skills at every level of the organization.

2

Rethinking Your Thinking

I become steadily more persuaded that perhaps the greatest disparity between reality and managerial perceptions is an underestimation of the potentialities of human beings for contributions to organizational effectiveness. These potentialities are not merely for increased expenditures of effort, but for the exercise of ingenuity, creativity in problem solving, acceptance of responsibility, leadership and the development of knowledge skills, and judgment.
—DOUGLAS McGREGOR, *The Professional Manager*

Every managerial act rests on assumptions, generalizations, and hypotheses—that is to say, on theory. Our assumptions are frequently implicit, sometimes quite unconscious, often conflicting; nevertheless, they determine our predictions that if we do *a*, *b* will occur. Theory and practice are inseparable. (*The Human Side of the Enterprise*, p. 6)

Douglas McGregor's most important legacy was neither Theory X nor Theory Y. It was his insistence that managers question their core assumptions about human nature, and that they see how these mental models lead to managerial practices. McGregor developed Theories X and Y to facilitate this questioning of our underlying assumptions. The problem with Theory X and Theory Y, however, is that McGregor labeled them as "theories," and most people in business have an aversion to such abstract terms. Therefore, they have turned these concepts into managerial styles. That is, people's natural resistance to question the way they think and their preoccupation with finding a simple method led them to misinterpret Theories X and Y as management practices or leadership styles (or *behaviors*) rather than as the assumptions and beliefs that McGregor intended.

As a result, even those managers who have attempted to follow McGregor's ideas have often failed to put his theories into practice. They have stopped short of his most important concern—that they question their own assumptions and beliefs. In fact, managers who familiarize themselves with Theories X and Y yet who fail to confront their true beliefs may be far more dangerous managers than those who have never heard of McGregor's work.

McGregor refused to simplify unbelievably organic and complex challenges into formulaic analyses and solutions. He believed that every situation was different: Like an individual person, the net result was a factor of countless variables. Yet leaders who look to implement his ideas still want easy answers—a simple, applicable, seven-step cure-all. They resist his message that every situation is unique and organic. In a self-fulfilling manner, many managers fail to implement his ideas because they believe them to be unimplementable. His ideas don't take hold because most managers don't believe they can put them into practice. When push comes to shove, most managers resist the hard work called for when managing people's values and motivations. They may want to have a conversation about it, but when it comes to dealing with people and organizations, they want something simple to use. This type of response plagued McGregor. In real life, the solutions to problems are far more complex and individual than any one generic response.

McGregor was often met with the following question: This is a great theory—but how do you make it work? And McGregor would invariably respond: "I don't know." He knew that his thinking worked only when each individual figured out how it worked *for them*. This explanation applies equally to McGregor's principles. People want a simple model they can implement effortlessly, regardless of who they are or what the unique situation demands. McGregor resisted such a simple response.

Above all, McGregor wanted people to look in the mirror and consider who they were and what they believe, a challenge that most people have at the very core of their being. And yet, until a person peels away the layers, looks at himself, and recognizes his deeply held beliefs and attitudes, he cannot lead or design a truly effective organization in today's world.

McGregor believed that organizations would be far more effective and powerful when managers offered employees the opportunity to align their individual goals with those of the business. His thinking reinforced the pragmatic message at the core of famed psychologist Abraham Maslow's work: People are capable of extraordinary accomplishments if they are able to meet their own self-fulfilling needs while pursuing the goals of the organization. Maslow referred to this approach as "enlightened management."

McGregor insisted on finding the theory animating practice. Without a theoretical basis, no managerial model can be truly effective. Take, for example, the scientific method. In the scientific method, we ask that you form a hypothesis before you test it out. Yet when managers are asked how do you motivate people or manage change, most people don't have a theory or a hypothesis.

A sales manager, for example, should ask what it takes to create loyalty with a client. What is the theory about this crucial business building block? Most people look for quantitative analysis or a recipe for techniques to link with customers. Yet the most important requirement may well be an emotional connection with the customer. Therefore, developing a working theory or hypothesis about what creates an emotional connection with customers would be valuable. Such a matter calls for a little theory, but not so much that we become paralyzed.

Douglas McGregor believed that the manager's set of assumptions and beliefs about the people he works with was seemingly endless: Why do they come to work? Will they seek responsibility in the right environment or is it more natural to shun responsibility? Must people be "jump started" for them to work hard? Will people commit to organizational goals without the use of individual incentives? Do people work well in groups or are they more affected when treated individually? Must people change their thinking before they will voluntarily change their behavior? Can we expect that people will leave their emotions at home or must they bring them to the workplace? Is behavior modification a useful motivational theory in an environment where innovation is key?

Coaching questions

And because, as he stated, "At the core of any theory of human resources are assumptions about human motivation," such assumptions must be brought to the surface and aligned with organizational practice. There is a clear and direct link between core assumptions (often hidden and tacit) and the working policies and practices of an organization. The performance appraisal system, for example, reflects the organization's beliefs about people. So does the compensation systems, the policies for sharing information, the systems by which decisions are made. Every operating practice in an organization emerges from the core beliefs of the individuals of that organization.

These beliefs determine practice whether they are explicit or implicit. Therefore, if we have a performance appraisal system that nobody agrees with or thinks is good or one that isn't fair, the fact that we perpetuate it must mean that we agree with or are afraid of something in that performance appraisal system. Managers who talk about intrinsic motivation but remain addicted to performance appraisal and compensation systems as a means of motivating employees agree, at some level, with the notion that people must be controlled and their behavior modified to get things done.

Leadership naturally reflects the assumptions and beliefs—the character—of the individual. In this human system of enterprise, leaders don't shape behavior by implementing consultant-driven models. Rather, they mobilize and align people through authenticity and presence. They realize that they cannot change the way they lead without trying to change the way they are. Their ability to move people in an organization derives not just from behavior but character—not just what you do but who you are. McGregor believed that you have to look in the mirror and figure out who you are because you can't lead in any other way. People change how they lead and manage only by changing who they are and how they think.

And yet the obstacles to following through on this simple concept are myriad. McGregor found that people do not have a good process for questioning and evaluating the way they think. Such a process was just too abstract for most. To do so would be to introduce a degree of uncertainty that is anathema to most take-charge managers. Questioning how they think would ask them to expose their weaknesses and exist in a realm that they couldn't necessarily master. It doesn't guarantee immediate and attainable results. Moreover, such a process is hard to justify in terms of risk factors. As management consultant Peter Drucker has argued, managers will not switch to new technologies until the benefits to be realized are exponentially higher than existing systems, as opposed to promising a mere one or two times advantage. This same principle applies to a managerial mindset. Comfortable managers, set in their stuck patterns, will not risk the switching costs of rethinking their thinking without a clear, demonstrable return on their time and emotion.

Dissertation measure this

> *Without a commitment to the development of human assets and without a clear understanding that providing for the growth of human resources is a painstaking and difficult task—but ultimately worth the effort—*

management must resort to recipes, fads, and
other "instance cures."
—DOUGLAS McGREGOR, *The Professional Manager*

The Costs of Hidden Theory

The consequences of this aversion have been huge. Rather than explore themselves, people in organizations turn to behavioral and contingency models that are easy to understand and easy to apply. For managers, these approaches represent a pragmatic solution. They play into their desire to use incentives and discipline to get people to act in ways that management outlined. They are easy to understand and easy to teach.

There is just one flaw: For the most part, these plans rarely engender significant change. They *do work* . . . but only in the short-term. Managers can control employees by bribing them with financial rewards. But that doesn't lead to greater commitment and innovation. It just provides a quick, yet fleeting, jolt in productivity. These measures are ultimately forms of compliance rather than commitment, and never lead to sustainable, qualitative improvement. People often leave training sessions as born-again managers and find that the behaviors that they are attempting to apply just don't work for them.

One of the most popular models that arose from this movement was the ABC model, which holds that attitudes lead to behavior, and behavior leads to consequences. This model mapped how people changed over time. The theory behind this plan was that people who changed their thinking would be more apt to change their behavior and, as a response, people who they worked with would read the intentions of the leader differently, and then respond differently. These plans assumed that managers could realize a better system by changing the surface behavior of the employees. Yet that would be akin to asking customer service representatives to deliver better service simply through establishing financial incentives rather than securing their commitment to provide truly satisfying service. Employees asked to achieve better quality, for example, would never realize dramatic results if they didn't buy in and begin learning the precepts, and thinking systematically as opposed to simply changing a few tactics.

These contingency models, which became addictive for many managers, spread a pernicious message: People in an organization react primarily to the behavior but not to the attitude and assumptions of the leader. These models taught that it was easier to change a person's behavior than it was to change their attitude. They ignored the importance of an employee's intrinsic commitment, believing instead that one's external actions are sufficient for peak performance.

Experience, however, has taught otherwise. First of all, a follower does not respond only to the behavior of the leader. People in organizations have great BS detectors. They perceive whether or not the leader is passionate about what they are talking about or merely spouting the party line. They know when a leader truly believes in the message he imparts, and when he is merely parroting orders from above.

More importantly, people can tell whether the leader cares about them or only cares about meeting his own goals and capturing the benefits of team performance. As followers, we look for respect, authenticity, honesty, and caring, and not just at the behaviors that a leader exhibits in a given situation. A leader who speaks a message of authenticity yet behaves in a manner inconsistent with these words sends the exact opposite message, just as any person in any relationship would. Think of a personal relationship in which we read the latest book and go home without changing our underlying belief system, yet try to behave in ways inconsistent with how we feel. To say, for example, "I love you" to someone else when you are not sure you do but feel you must, invariably sounds hollow to the other person. It can feel insulting, which is clearly not the desired consequence. No matter how an individual acts, behavior exhibited in an attempt to get something in return will appear manipulative and feel insincere. Manipulation under any name erodes trust and is detrimental to the long-term development of relationships.

Any leader should seriously examine his or her personal motives and assumptions, when asking others to follow her lead. She must monitor if her message is truly aligned with what she believes. This could involve asking questions such as: Am I doing this because I want something in return or because I care? Do I really believe in delegation and participation or is it the latest technique I am trying in order to get what I need? Do I trust people or am I trying to act like I trust people? Do I really want to involve people or do I want them to feel like they are involved?

Second, leaders with enough power to force people to change their behavior can more quickly change that behavior by educating them and sharing learning to help people reflect and update their assumptions. This is a far more effective and authentic force of change than coercion, incentives, or persuasion.

In the short-term, a leader can affect change by bribing an employee, or threatening to fire an employee. But at what cost? People who are manipulated or coerced do not commit to change easily. We have all experienced this. Push people to change, and in most cases, we simply increase the resistance to change. Anything that lowers people's feeling of control will almost universally create pushback. Leaders can force short-term behavioral changes—but short-term is the operative idea. Most contingency theorists hope that the experience of the change will lower people's resistance to the unknown. Undoubtedly that happens at times. We try the new behavior and we like it. But it has been our experience that the more likely reaction is one of defensiveness and resistance that lowers learning and inhibits change.

The bottom line is that the ABC model is a better working hypothesis than one that emphasizes a BC loop (i.e., try on the behavior, get the consequence, and then change the behavior without substantially rethinking the underlying assumptions). This is especially true when we need more than mere compliance. Consider the business challenge of providing world-class service. Companies that seek to better this function often survey their customers on satisfaction, and tie employee pay to that number. This rarely improves how people work; rather it gives them an incentive to rig the survey numbers. They'll bribe customers who buy a car to complete the survey positively.

They'll find ways to trick people into giving them high ratings. It's a cycle of bribery in which people want better survey results. And the sad truth is that they don't care more about the customers. There's a crucial difference between somebody trying to be the best they can be, and somebody scheming to score the highest number.

In a business system driven by surveys and extrinsic motivations, employees will spend far more time and energy manipulating the boss's perception than dealing with the customer's true satisfaction.

McGregor believed that a business could not be run on mere mechanics—that every element of the human resources policy had to be examined at the core rather than simply analyzed to see what appeared to be most effective. Likewise, McGregor held that it was far more important to completely rethink performance appraisal or think more systemically, as a means of rethinking *who you were,* rather than trying to fix a new performance appraisal system.

Between the Theory and the Practice Falls the Shadow

*Theory X and Theory Y are not managerial
strategies. They are underlying beliefs about
the nature of man that influence managers to
adopt one strategy rather than another.*
—DOUGLAS McGREGOR, *The Professional Manager*

If you were to ask managers which operating model shaped their choices and policies, most would say that they believe in the tenets of Theory Y. Yet if you were to look at their working polices and practices, you would see that their actions are more consistent with Theory X. Most people are tempted to think of themselves as one or the other. The real question is not whether you are Theory X or Theory Y. These contrasting theories were neither styles nor ways of being, but simple constructs to test one's core assumptions. The more pressing matter is: Why can't you realize a more system-oriented participative type of management?

Is it because we think these theories of management belong in a lab? Or because we say you don't know the kind of people working here? Or you can't hold me accountable for that type of performance if I can't control the people? Or how can I get those sales guys to sell so hard if I don't have the right incentive to offer them? We say all those things but don't really think about them. If I *say* these things, this is what I really believe.

In corporations you often hear take-charge managers refer to the employees in their company as "My People." They intend this term to be one of endearment, one that indicates how close they are, but in most cases they are revealing something far different. If you were to ask: "When you say *my people,* does that mean that you own them?" these same managers would snap back: "No, of course I don't." But there is a critical distinction. These words have power. Those who think of people as "theirs" tend to consider these possessions as something to be controlled. And those who talk of being part of a team tend to also value a more humane culture.

When People Use Theory Y to Behave Like Theory X

> *We say that an important reason for group*
> *consideration of important decisions is to get*
> *the benefit of different points of view. Yet, by*
> *denying or suppressing the emotional factors*
> *which are among the major causes of different*
> *points of view, we defeat our stated purposes.*
> —DOUGLAS McGREGOR, The Professional Manager

In a recent consulting position, we were asked to address the topic of moving from a command-and-control culture to one that is more entrepreneurial, innovative, and empowered. We assumed that the people who asked us to speak on this topic would live by these values. Yet in planning the speech, we began receiving phone calls inquiring about our talk. We were given a list of words we were expected to use and models we would abide by. A vice president met with us to make sure that we wouldn't say anything contrary to his beliefs. And when we told these executives about feeling overmanaged and controlled, they replied defensively, saying that they thought they were good with people. But they were going to force people to be more empowered and entrepreneurial. They didn't see the problem with the way they were trying to bring about a new culture—the process of the change project was in fact the content, and that this content was the same old way.

It is always easier to check our assumptions using a practice than by looking in the mirror and asking if we think people are trustworthy. Most managers like to believe that their personal beliefs are closer to Theory Y than Theory X. However, when many of these same managers are asked to evaluate their organizational structures, they find the actual practices contain the vestiges of an old, mechanistic organization with a decidedly Theory X tint.

What's Your Working Theory?

This exercise is designed to help find the discrepancy between what you think you do and what you actually do. Look at your present practices and examine, for example, why you believe that if you take away incentives people won't work as hard. Or that you need to treat managers different from the front line, or that in service companies the front-line person never gathers the information. You may believe that you are operating by Theory X principles, but instead behavior modification—a system far more consistent with Theory Y beliefs—animates your working system. Let's look at the assumptions behind the system by which you manage. Ask yourself the following questions:

- Pick a management practice that we now use that we believe to be problematic.
- Determine the purpose for which the practice exists.
- What are the underlying assumptions that the originators would have had in developing this process?
- Are they consistent with what we believe happens in human organizations?
- What are the potential unintended consequences of this process?

It's easy to mistake Theory X for an autocratic screaming manager. The *apparent* behavior of an organization often disguises the true beliefs hidden within. A kind, paternalistic, incentive-laden culture can be and usually is built on the belief that people must be enticed to work because committing themselves in the working environment is not a natural act for most people in certain types of jobs.

If we perpetuate a practice that is consistent with a set of assumptions about people, we will wear those assumptions whether or not we personally believe that they are us. We are the values of the organization to those who work there. If we want people to react to what we think, we need to ensure that there is consistency in the environment and the structures of the organization.

Conversation with Jim Collins

Jim Collins, author of "Built to Last: Successful Habits of Visionary Companies," *believes that Douglas McGregor's most important legacy to current management is his insistence that all managers identify their theory of human behavior, and then align their organizational practice accordingly.*

McGregor's stand that managers should analyze their theory is more profound and powerful than his creation of Theory X and Theory Y. Chester Bernard also talked about aligning individual and organizational goals.

"*What's so powerful is the observation that the world operates by a social psychology principle known as the fundamental attribution error. This argues that the assumptions that a power figure brings into a situation will be a self-fulfilling prophecy. If a teacher believes that the students don't want to learn, for example, that will become a self-fulfilling prophecy. That professor may attribute a lack of learning orientation to the students when, in fact, this condition is a belief held by the professor. And in fact, that professor will then behave toward his students in such a manner that this belief naturally becomes manifest.*

"*This principle holds true for the 'swing group' in an organization. That is, those people whose motivations and beliefs can be influenced by the environment in which they work. There are those on either end who will be positive or negative regardless. That is, there will be some people who will always be lazy, and some who are intrinsically motivated despite any heed of X or Y. McGregor's message is powerful in direct proportion to the size of the swing group. The swing group in mediocre organizations is a much larger percentage; in great organizations it is very small.*

"Today many organizations try to live by the principles of Theory Y. That is, their operating practices reflect a more positive view of human nature. And yet, and this is the key, many of these companies still haven't put in place the notion of theory as a fundamental tool in creating managerial practice. I think Theory Y is a very valuable thing to put in place. But if you could get people shifting to the practice of using theory as a managerial tool, that would be great, too."

3 | Becoming McGregorian

*I am of the firm belief that the capacity for
self-actualization, which is so obvious in the
small child, remains in the adult, even though
it may be latent because of environmental
restraints. I see a genuine potential for a
linkage of self-actualization with
organizational goals. Strategy planning that
takes into account this assumed human
characteristic can lead to a more effective
organization in sheer economic terms.*
—DOUGLAS McGREGOR, *The Professional Manager*

Douglas McGregor's beliefs in what motivated people and how managers were responsible for recognizing and developing this creative force within their employees was unheard of in his day—and have even now only been partially implemented. His ideas about the true essence of people in the workplace and his unwavering commitment to creating a new set of values for guiding the spirit of the workplace was considered heresy by some and an epiphany by others. McGregor's willingness and ability to challenge the norm continues to inspire managers to new

levels of organizational excellence and provides a set of values that res-
onates with employees.

McGregor challenged management's assumptions that:

1. Only management was responsible for the economic success of the company;
2. People needed to be controlled and their behavior modified to fit the needs of the organization;
3. Without control by management, people would be passive—even resistant—to the company's needs; and
4. The average worker is by nature indolent, he will work as little as possible and needs to be led.

McGregor further proposed that the traditional aspects of the organization—its structure, practices, and policies—reinforced negative
assumptions about what motivates people. Instead, McGregor believed
that people in the workplace could be held to a higher degree of motivation. McGregor challenged the managers of his day to hold their beliefs up to the harsh light of scrutiny. He urged them to accept, as he
did, the notion that if people were passive, they became so as a result of
their experience in the company, and, more importantly, that the capacity for people to accept increased responsibility is the obligation of
management. It is up to the manager to recognize and develop these attributes in their workforce; and it is the responsibility of the employee
to seek out greater satisfaction through work. Like McGregor, the authors believe that both managers and their employees need to embrace
the challenges of work to achieve Theory Y actualization—where employees take responsibility for their growth and leaders better understand the conditions under which this growth can be nurtured.

In his writing and teaching, McGregor emphasized that work was a
process for creating opportunities, unlocking potential, encouraging
growth, and offering guidance. This book—and this section in particular—provides managers with a new mental model and challenges their
opinions, beliefs, and assumptions about the behavior of people in the

workplace. The concepts of active participation, concern with individual dignity and growth, and aligning individual needs with organizational goals were challenges that McGregor defined over 40 years ago. These ideas have become even more relevant today. This section introduces a new set of challenges for managers, posing questions that in the true spirit of being McGregorian may be difficult—even uncomfortable—to answer. These challenges must be addressed if organizations and their leaders hold any hope of internalizing those attributes that McGregor held so dearly.

Where Everyone Is a Knowledge Worker

> *The more affluent the society, the more significant will be meaningful careers. People will perceive job opportunities as a way to pursue their goals in membership in such formal organizations with whose goals they can link their own.*
>
> —DOUGLAS McGREGOR, *The Professional Manager*

In a McGregorian world, where there is a direct correlation between how much you know about your customer and your company and the strength of the relationships you create, every worker will have to be a *knowledge* worker. This term, which has become commonplace in today's business vocabulary, holds at its essence those beliefs about which McGregor was so passionate. For knowledge workers, jobs as we know them have been replaced by an employment contract, which rewards those managers and their employees who take personal responsibility for bringing value to the organization and adding merit to the work they perform. No longer will job descriptions merely outline the tasks to be performed by employees. Instead, employees and their managers will be expected to do whatever is necessary to achieve the single overarching outcome that will determine the success or failure of their organization: creating loyal relationships with customers, suppliers, and colleagues. Rather than judging a person's success or failure by individual tasks—irrespective of the larger result—employees will be able to gauge their value to the enterprise by their ability to create and nurture relationships.

Participative management, knowledge workers, open-book management, values-based management, workgroups, and the democratic workplace were visions McGregor had for the world of business. The challenges that follow are designed to make McGregor's thinking come alive today within the organization. Analyzing the challenges that follow and assessing yourself against these ideals will help you create the belief system needed to become McGregorian.

The Challenges of Leadership

> *The "good society," whatever form it may take, will be created only by organized human effort. An affluent and more highly educated population will seek intrinsic rewards in the pursuit of new goals, in the innovative solution of new problems. New organizations and new institutions will need to be created for these purposes.*
>
> —DOUGLAS McGREGOR, *The Professional Manager*

In a McGregorian world—and now more than ever before—we must work to create a culture where loyalty to the company's stakeholders (shareholders, employees, suppliers, and customers) supersedes all other loyalties. To this culture, we must bring a vision—our own and the collective shared vision of everyone in the workforce. No longer can this vision be imposed from above as if by divine will, but it must be arrived at mutually—or people won't follow it. Managers must concentrate their efforts on building a day-to-day work environment where values are practiced on a consistent basis and held in the highest regard and where risk is not only tolerated, but encouraged.

To unleash the full potential of the workforce and earn the commitment of our co-workers, we must fight against the preconceived idea shared by many that employees don't want responsibility; they don't want to know more, learn more, be accountable for more. This will be a difficult battle, however, because there is more than an element of truth in this notion. How so? Because in the mass-production, simple-job/complex-process model, responsibility usually involves risk taking and sometimes failure, which employees have learned must be avoided at any cost, even if it leads to mediocre performance and lackluster results. In a McGregorian world, however, mediocre performance and lackluster results are untenable. Risk and failure are part of the territory not punishable by anything worse than the opportunity to try again, using what was learned the first time to improve our chances of success in subsequent attempts.

To those of us in business today, the value of unleashing the human potential of our co-workers and employees is hardly news. If our rhetoric is any indication, we all know how important employees are—particularly those on the front line—to building the strong relationships we must maintain with our loyal stakeholders to keep from becoming obsolete.

We know that, whether we're delivering health care, writing software, or manufacturing electronic equipment, if we are to thrive in the new economy—where relationships are king and products and services are custom-made—the mousetrap will only be as good as the path that leads us there. Managers must require a staff that is more than a compliant workforce that checks its brains at the door and puts in its time. On the contrary, managers need to hire and nurture employees committed to building that relationship, sharing a collective vision for doing so, and creating exceptional value for each individual along the way.

Motivated, involved, and committed employees can result in a lower cost of doing business, higher productivity, substantial process improvement, faster service innovations, better customer information, new employee referrals, and much more. Lately, too, many of us are acknowledging, even advertising our commitment to employees: "Our people," we claim, "are our most important asset." In fact, just ask any of us how important it is for our organization to have the day-in and day-out commitment of the men and women on the job, and chances are excellent that our answer will be concise and to the point: "Absolutely critical."

But, if the commitment of our co-workers is as critical as we say it is, how do we win that commitment? What will keep our workforce loyal, creative, and excited? To these questions, we're often slower to respond. And when we do, our answers are almost always identical to those surrounding customer loyalty and commitment: "It depends," we say. It depends on the individual employees and who they are. It depends on their needs and expectations. It depends on what excites them about work, and what programs and systems can be devised to keep them that way.

The Lincoln Electric Company (Cleveland, OH) is a leading manufacturer of arc welding and cutting products and has been so for over a century. A billion dollar firm, Lincoln is best known for its progressive management system that holds at its core those qualities that McGregor emphasized in his teaching and writing. At Lincoln, trust is the lynchpin to their management systems, tying together five interrelated qualities that make up the company's organizational design: commitment, conflict management, learning, systems thinking, and agility. Although these five variables are highly interdependent, trust is the key. Once high levels of trust exist in the organization, employee commitment is gained. The open environment fostered by trust and commitment enables the company to manage conflict in a way that is constructive without destroying loyal relationships. Learning happens as employees work through problem-solving situations within the context of cross-functional teams and their general responsibilities. Systems thinking is furthered by these same teams, as well as by job rotation and extensive communication between management and employees. Finally, what brings these five elements to life is a combination of executive leadership and formalized management systems. Lincoln's leadership style, culture, and management systems combine to create an environment that mobilizes employees and creates the type of intrinsically motivating and rewarding environment that McGregor envisioned.

Personalizing the Workplace

Meaningful work is an important part of a satisfactory life and the degree to which work provides opportunities for intrinsic rewards is important to the survival of the organization.
—DOUGLAS McGREGOR, *The Professional Manager*

As human beings, we all actively seek out personalized treatment. We appreciate being treated as individuals; we hate being treated as part of the mass. We like being listened to, understood, respected, and we're angry when our requests are trivialized or ignored. But, if we genuinely believe that employees have the same human needs as we do and that the only way to win their commitment is by treating them each as individuals, are the people practices we have in our organizations up to the task? Can we get to where we say we want to go with the systems we have in place? Is what we think about employees consistent with what we say about or to them? Pose these questions to virtually anyone who works in a medium- to large-size organization and you're likely to encounter skepticism. Our words say that we're ready to put aside our mass mentality in dealing with employees and take the leap into what we've described as a McGregorian world. Most of what we say indicates that we've already taken that leap, and that we're well under way. In many instances, however, our actions suggest otherwise.

Examining Our Practices

Those influences which give the illusion but not the fact are manipulative. They are expressed sometimes in managerial circles by phrases like "make them feel important" and "give them a sense of participation." Open,

*admitted coercive influences are far more
desirable. My reasons are both ethical and
practical. The ethical one is obvious. The
practical reason concerns the danger of backfire
when the manipulation is recognized. The
resultant mistrust is likely to be long lived
and difficult to overcome.*

—DOUGLAS McGREGOR, *The Professional Manager*

It's time we face the facts. While company after company claims that its
employees are its most important asset, the majority of employee policies and practices don't bear this out. If we genuinely believe that employees are our number one asset and that the only way to win their
individual commitment is by treating them as individuals, how can we
expect them to take us seriously when we continue to rely on one-size-
fits-all people practices? For example, job descriptions narrowly define
the scope of work and rarely consider the scope of the individual's real
talents and personal aspirations. Performance appraisals group individual employees into one of five boxes, pretending it's fair, pretending it's
objective, and pretending the employees will learn and benefit from the
experience. What about compensation systems that focus on getting
people to do what we want rather than improving the process or encouraging learning and growth?

If we really cared about employees and were serious about them as
individuals, wouldn't we develop a growth path for each of them that
encompasses what that person wants or needs from his or her tenure
with us? After all, if employees can't attain their personal goals at work,
how can we expect them to commit to the job? If employees are truly
our most important asset, why is it that the training budget is the first
thing cut when money gets tight? And why is our first concern in developing a policy not usually whether it's good for the workforce but
whether it's legally defensible? If we genuinely wanted employees to
give us their best, wouldn't we do our best to ensure that they have the
skills and knowledge necessary to do so? Failing that, wouldn't we at
least want to know if they are married, have a family, have problems or

concerns away from the workplace that we could perhaps help with, to win their respect and trust as well as their commitment? To treat them as human beings with individual emotions and concerns and not just as human resources?

The problem today is that it's a rare company, and an exceptional leader, who dares to devote the time and effort to form the human relationships with co-workers that lead to the commitment we all say we're looking for. In place of these relationships—particularly in larger companies—we tend to create one-size-fits-all systems to "handle" employees—practices and policies that are clearly throwbacks to yesterday's mass mentality.

If we are serious about meeting the challenges of a McGregorian world, we must look in the mirror and learn from our past efforts. We must make unleashing the potential of people a strategic imperative and we must commit to finding a better way.

At Lincoln Electric, the overall key to producing trust and commitment within the company and infusing these qualities into the management system is the values established by both the words and actions of their leaders. Values that produce the results we have seen at Lincoln are viewed by its workforce as just and moral. These values have historically been both stated and demonstrated by top management.

Getting On with the Job

> The ingenuity and the perseverance of
> industrial management in the pursuit of
> economic ends have changed many scientific
> and technological dreams into commonplace
> realities. It is now becoming clear that the
> application of these same talents to the human
> side of enterprise will not only enhance
> substantially these materialistic achievements
> but will bring us one step closer to the "good
> society." Shall we get on with the job?
> —DOUGLAS McGREGOR, The Professional Manager

How can we learn to help our workforce add value in a McGregorian world? How do you build an environment in which people will seek responsibility, search for better answers, and be willing and able to reach their full potential? How do you motivate employees?

Before he died in 1964, M.I.T. Professor Douglas McGregor repeatedly asked students and managers this very question: "How do you motivate employees?" In posing the question, he was not looking for a specific answer but asking how the process can be improved and learning encouraged.

Because McGregor didn't believe that a simple answer existed, he attempted to get each manager to articulate an idea about what might entice people to make a maximum contribution at work. In his attempt to help managers articulate hypotheses, McGregor frequently came up empty. And the theories that people did put forth, theories like "reward success/punish failure," often didn't mix with the personal beliefs about human nature these people professed. If managers and students had theories, they were usually incomplete, frequently unexamined, and, in some cases, riddled with internal contradictions. What McGregor encountered nearly four decades ago is probably not much different from what he might encounter today. Although most managers agree that leading people is their primary job, most have not developed a hypothesis about how to go about unleashing the potential of people. And, if they have, it's more than likely they haven't subjected this theory to rigorous examination. What has been examined—with great rigor—are the numbers: If the numbers are good, the thinking goes, so is the theory; if they aren't, it's time to try another theory.

Theory into Action

We are, by and large, a practical people. We prefer practice to theory and action to exploration; at times, we have little patience with ideas that cannot be practically applied *now*. In many cases, our predilection to action has served us well. But, in our efforts to create a work environment in which people can excel, our aversion to theory and to examining the consequences of our assumptions has often led us to perpetuate practices that, rather than motivating people, undermine them. If we are to capture the creativity, imagination, and best efforts of people, we have no choice but to explore the impact our theories have on the men and women we are counting on to carry the day in an actualizing and profitable business world. In other words, without theory, even our best efforts are left unexamined and are bound to fall short.

Humans, Not Machines

I become steadily more persuaded that perhaps the greatest disparity between objective reality and managerial perceptions of it is an underestimation of the potentialities of human beings for contributions to organizational effectiveness. These potentialities are not merely for increased expenditure of effort on limited jobs (although such potentialities do exist) but for the exercise of ingenuity; creativity in problem solving; acceptance of responsibility; leadership in the relational sense; and development of knowledge, skill, and judgment. When opportunities are provided under appropriate conditions, managers are regularly astonished to discover how much more people contribute than they had believed possible.

—DOUGLAS McGREGOR, *The Professional Manager*

The major thrust of McGregor's writing about motivation was that managers seeking to unleash human potential must first abandon their oversimplified, mechanistic view of the workplace and learn to deal with the human side of the organization. No longer could employees be thought of as machine parts to be fixed, redesigned, or eliminated if problems arose. Instead, employees would have to be treated as individuals, in all their complexity.

Putting McGregor's thinking into practice, however, as many of us know, is easier said than done. Even though most managers will quickly agree that people are more complex than machines, the systems that we inherited from the days of mass production and scientific management are often based on the assumption that people are no more than an extension of the over-specialized, over-engineered process in which they work. Furthermore, the goal of these systems and the practices they spawned wasn't to get people to think, only to follow orders. And, with enough power, getting people to comply was not that complicated a task.

While these simple, mechanically based systems may be sufficient to obtain obedience to work rules and compliance to processes, they do little to improve the relationship with the workers we need to gain their commitment or stimulate a more learning-oriented culture. In fact, implementing and perpetuating these practices often distract us from the kind of experimentation and analysis required to understand how better to interact with individuals and groups of individuals. In trying to control more effectively or manage more predictably, we are robbing ourselves of countless opportunities to learn how to be more effective leaders.

Lessons of Lasting Value at Lincoln Electric

The main characteristics that differentiate Lincoln Electric from the majority of other organizations are:

- The reservoir of trust that has been developed between the company's management and workers.
- Trust at Lincoln has been established through formal and informal communications between labor and management.
- Serving the customer has always been the way to economic security for labor and management.
- Continuous employee development and continuous improvement in quality and productivity have always played a dominant role in the company's management processes.
- Continuous employment is earned and not awarded in a paternalistic manner.
- The company's management systems and processes are in tune with the realities and the needs of human nature.
- Employees are rewarded based upon productivity and quality of output. Gainsharing exists along side of painsharing.
- Management takes responsibility for assuring that the company grows and can continue to provide good jobs for the people who have demonstrated that they are productive and reliable.

These are the principles and practices upon which Lincoln has been established.

(Reprinted with the permission of John Wiley & Sons, 2000, *Lasting Value: Lessons from a Century of Agility at Lincoln Electric* by Joseph Maciariello.)

4 | Thinking Systematically

Much of the behavior we see today in typical industrial organizations is not a consequence of human nature; it is a consequence of the way we organize, of the way we manage people.

—DOUGLAS McGREGOR, *The Professional Manager*

Albert Einstein told us, "How we think determines what we measure." It also determines how we organize and how we do business. Our thinking, our belief system, our mindset determines our priorities, our procedures, our processes, what we expect from people, and the way we deal with them. A distillation of our past thoughts, observations, and experience, our mindset serves as the foundation for the systems we build and perpetuate.

This may sound somewhat theoretical, but it's theory that works. If you hope to sustain your success in the future or change your current practices, you must examine the thinking that underlies what you do and how your organization behaves. Before we can create the type of company we desire—the fast, flexible one populated by loyal employees and driven by loyal customers—we must ensure that our mindset will support it. We simply can't think one thing and do another, and expect to do either very well.

Our mindset is enormously valuable. It enables us to act. Without it we would have no way to relate yesterday's events and problems to today's, no basis for our predictions, no framework for organizing information, and little confidence in our actions. Without a set of assumptions to guide our actions, every management decision we make, no matter how slight, would take forever. We would have to weigh every variable and ponder every possible outcome. Without a basic set of beliefs to guide us, every decision would be our first.

On the other hand, with a belief system we trust, we can make assumptions about cause and effect, build models to describe how the world works, be confident in our solutions, and generally bring order to the complexities inherent in managing an organization.

foundation for a coaching model

The biggest problem with a mindset is that once we've developed one, we tend not to challenge it, particularly when it seems effective. Why should we? If it worked yesterday and works today, it should work tomorrow, right? Not necessarily. Not even probably. In fact, in a rapidly changing environment such as the one we compete in today, leaping to this conclusion is dangerous business. Instead, to ensure that our thinking does not become outdated, we must continuously put our old ideas to the test, to question the efficacy of yesterday's truths and do so *before* they fail.

Having a certain mindset can also be problematic for the leader if, when setting new organizational goals and developing new tactics, he or she doesn't go back to question whether the assumptions underlying that mindset are consistent with the company's new direction. If our beliefs are consistent with our new aspirations, chances are that, as we try to change the organization, we'll create structures that will prompt the desired performance. If, however, our beliefs are not aligned with what we're trying to accomplish, our mindset will become an invisible barrier to improvement. All of us in the workplace must continually re-examine the way we think.

Coaching creates a space for this to occur

Subjecting our mindset to a rigorous re-examination is often easier said than done. Our beliefs are abstractions, hard to pin down and articulate. More than likely, we never commit them to paper, we're rarely

in a situation in which we have to defend them, and we seldom have
the inclination to question them. In many cases, we don't even know
where our beliefs came from or how they originated—they are just an
amalgamation of our experience over time. Still, they come into play
every day, with every decision we make, which in turn continues to
influence the way people in the organization behave.

Systems thinking at Lincoln Electric begins with a clear focus on
how to create value for the customer. This leads to analyzing how employees can be incented to attain customer value. The management systems at Lincoln are then designed to appeal to all of the higher level
qualities in the workforce—morality, dignity, rationality, creativity,
mastery, and community—to satisfy customers (and employees) on a
continuous basis.

Articulate, Question, and Debate

Behind every attempt to influence others lies
a theory (or a belief or a conviction)
concerning cause and effect in human
behavior.
—DOUGLAS McGREGOR, *The Professional Manager*

What McGregor suggested and what we now know is that examining
and updating our thinking will take a combination of guts and forth-
rightness. The best place to start is by articulating the assumptions we
feel are necessary for the future success of our organization. Most probably, this will require that we put our own beliefs to the test by sharing
them with others. Until we do, little progress can be made in determining whether our beliefs are serving us well. On the other hand, if
we let our beliefs go unarticulated, they can become counterproductive
to the organization—difficult to question, difficult to create a dialogue
about, difficult to test. This can lead to a perpetuation of those beliefs
through generations of employees without our assumptions ever facing
the scrutiny they deserve.

A cautionary note: Being only human, many of us tend to protect our beliefs (usually unintentionally), rather than genuinely examining them. Indeed, to a greater or lesser degree, we all protect the way we think. Typically this takes the form of:

- Interpreting information in a manner that is consistent with past beliefs.
- Rationalizing conflicting information and discounting the validity of inconsistent data.
- Actively seeking out reinforcing information.
- Hiring people with similar mindsets (because obviously, they are the best qualified).
- Aggressively challenging conflicting views when they are expressed.
- Creating structures where being right is more important than learning.
- Defining our role as advocate of a position instead of a learning partner in the process.
- Punishing mistakes, which makes it more difficult to experiment with different ways of thinking and acting.
- Not developing the skills it takes to question present ways of thinking or to learn from new experiences.

As unproductive as some of these behaviors may seem, in many organizations they are often tacitly, if not openly, rewarded. Our organizations would be very different if, instead of supporting these behaviors, we were held accountable for offering insightful answers to the following questions:

- What have I learned lately?
- In the last six months, what have I changed my mind about?
- When was the last time my assumptions were dead wrong?
- What is different about the way I think this year?
- What about my present mindset do I find myself questioning recently?

- What have I learned this month that makes my actions last month seem less effective?
- Who thinks very differently than I do? What have I learned from them lately?
- How much time have I spent in the last month questioning the way I think and the structures I have designed to support improvement?

Continuously testing the quality of our thinking must become a fundamental part of every improvement process. Inevitably, articulating, sharing, and questioning assumptions will raise issues about what makes a successful organization. These issues should be discussed among diverse groups to ensure that a wide range of opinions and contrary points of view are heard. We should then take what we learn from these discussions to redesign the way work is done and eliminate any inconsistencies we uncover. If we don't, we'll create a heap of cynicism that will not only destroy enthusiasm but, even more important, undermine trust.

By definition, any discussion of what, why, and how we think will focus more on theory than action. As system architects and leaders responsible for a highly complex structure, we have no choice but to ensure that the foundation we are working from can support what we hope to build.

Through its formal and informal management systems and its emphasis on open communication, Lincoln Electric constantly re-evaluates the effectiveness of processes, programs, and policies. This constant analysis and subsequent modification of the organization's operations to meet marketplace demands can be strongly credited in Lincoln Electric's 100+ years of growth and profitability.

5

Performance Appraisal or Performance Development

Managers are uncomfortable when they are put in the position of "playing God." The respect we hold for the inherent value of the individual leaves us distressed when we must take responsibility for judging the personal worth of a fellow man.
—DOUGLAS McGREGOR, *The Professional Manager*

Throughout this section, we've talked about the structures and assumptions whose unintended effects often undermine teamwork, inhibit experimentation and learning, encourage mediocrity, and stifle creativity and innovation. Nowhere are these effects more readily apparent than in the performance appraisal process practiced by so many organizations today. This is the process that McGregor took the most exception to. In his classic article, "An Uneasy Look at Performance Appraisals,"

McGregor suggests new ways managers can approach the performance appraisal process. Managers for the first time are introduced to those qualities that we now categorize as *mentoring*. This classic work has been reprinted in Part 2 of the book.

About performance appraisal, there are currently many more questions than answers. Are performance appraisal methods fair? Accurate? What are the effects of a forced distribution process?

Should compensation be tied to appraisal results? Is past performance a valid indicator of future performance, particularly when the job changes significantly? Will positive feedback from an appraisal lead to higher levels of performance? Are the methods used to measure the effectiveness of performance appraisal themselves effective?

Of all the questions raised by performance appraisal systems, the single most compelling, we feel, is whether their primary purpose is evaluative or developmental; that is, are they a grading tool or a learning tool? The answer in most organizations is: both—however, the vast majority of cases are evaluative. This leads to a second question . . . and a third: Can a single system perform twin functions? And, as currently designed, is the performance appraisal process particularly effective at doing either? Our experience suggests that, in most cases, the answer to both these questions is no.

With the best of intentions, leaders in almost every organization have tried to develop systems that provide fair, honest feedback to help employees learn, while providing information that managers need to differentiate among performance levels and reward individuals or teams accordingly. When learning and evaluation are combined into one system, however, a single overarching problem inevitably arises: the problem of the boss as both evaluator and coach.

To really learn and develop, people must be able to share weaknesses as well as strengths and must view information about their present performance as hopeful and nonthreatening. However, in a process where one individual is both evaluator and coach, can we really assume that employees will be truly candid in discussing their weaknesses? Probably not.

Distinguishing the Indistinguishable

*The modern emphasis upon the manager as a
leader who strives to help his subordinates
achieve both their own and the company's
objectives is hardly consistent with the judicial
role demanded by most appraisal plans.*
—DOUGLAS McGREGOR, *The Professional Manager*

In forced distribution evaluation processes, the frustration of trying to differentiate individuals where no major differences exist has led many a manager to take imaginative steps.

As an evaluative tool, performance appraisal is generally used to; rate performance, skills, and experience for compensation purposes serve as a basis for rewards and recognition; and provide a foundation for promotion practices. Often, too, performance evaluations are meant to motivate employees to perform better in the hope of getting a better evaluation (or for fear of getting a negative one) next time.

The problem, almost everyone in the organization will agree, is that the information generated in most performance evaluation systems is incomplete at best and can frequently be misleading. Also, aside from one or two top performers or one or two poor performers, it is exceedingly difficult to differentiate among individual performances. In many cases, too, the erroneous assumption is made that the performance of an individual can be isolated from the overall performance of the department and organization. Even if the information gathered in performance evaluations was accurate, its negative, unintended effects would still be reason to seriously question the viability and value of its use. Chief among these effects is the fact that competition is inherent in performance evaluation systems and that appraisals weigh individuals against each other and force them to compete for a limited number of wins. Performance appraisal, therefore, can result in many of the same problems that arise from competition, including:

- A scarcity mentality that inhibits cooperation and teamwork.
- Stifled creativity and innovation.
- Reduced efficiencies and compromised product and service quality.
- Inhibited dialogue.
- Demoralized "losers" and destroyed self-esteem resulting in compromised relationships.

Performance appraisal can shift the focus of the employee from the customer to the boss. When your future depends on one individual's perception of you, managing that person's perception becomes key. As much rhetoric as there is in organizations today about teamwork and customer focus, with performance appraisal in the balance, the boss becomes the number one focus—particularly because instances where a boss can measure an employee's ability or performance are so infrequent. While this may serve to reaffirm the boss's status in the organization, it does little in the way of increasing cooperation, and even less for enhancing the value that can be delivered to customers. We've all been to meetings where the primary concern of most people in the room was to please the boss—even if it meant displeasing the customer.

Performance appraisal can encourage mediocrity. Whenever evaluation is part of the process and the results of the evaluation can affect your career, the tendency is to negotiate for goals you know you can easily meet, rather than ones that require experimentation or new processes where the possibility of mistakes or failures are greater. And woe be to us if we negotiate for true stretch goals and succeed. Since then, more than likely, next year's goals will be set substantially higher—often without an analysis of whether the goal is even achievable. Since the price of failure is often high, better to be realistic in our negotiations and set goals that *appear* to be a stretch but aren't really. In this way, while the absolute level of our performance may be mediocre (i.e., substantially similar to that of others) it can still serve us well in our careers.

Performance appraisal can reduce and pervert information flow. If you're reluctant to talk about things gone wrong, problem areas, or experiments that may fail for fear that the information will be used against you in your performance evaluation, all that is left to talk about are the positives. This results in a rose-colored glasses view of the organization that leaves bosses at every level with progressively more distorted pictures of reality.

Performance appraisal can create a short-term focus. Because of high job turnover and rapid rotation rates, managers are usually most concerned with performance improvements that can be demonstrated during their tenure. Also, because the duration of an evaluation is typically no more than a year, the tendency of many being evaluated is to tailor their performance to that same time period, rather than thinking of their jobs as a continuous, evolving endeavor. And because memories are short, appraisals done in December may ignore the successes of March or April and focus on the failures of October and November.

Performance appraisals can undermine organizational vision and values. A manager can talk about a vision, can paint it clearly, write the most eloquent vision statement, then cause nothing but confusion if the achievements of the people promoted and rewarded do not reflect that vision. The measures that provide the basis of many performance appraisals do not describe performance adequately. Too often, evaluations are based on what is easy to measure or has been traditionally measured, whether the person made the boss look good, or whether the person is perceived as a team player. When a person is promoted because of an outstanding evaluation, many others will try to emulate that person's behavior. If there is a disjunction between that behavior and the one articulated in the vision, there is little question which behavior will be mimicked.

Performance appraisal can destroy trust. Simply put, to base someone's future on forced rationalizations and "knockout criteria" is embarrassing for the manager who has to do it and unfair to the employee to whom it is done. It may be possible to differentiate between your highest and lowest performer. But what about all those in between, particularly those you don't have frequent contact with? And how do you differentiate among those whose efforts you support and those you don't? For the individuals on the receiving end who garner anything but the highest rating, the first response is usually frustration (if not anger) followed by disappointment, and ultimately by a lack of trust in the organization (and, by extension, its leaders) that underwrites what is perceived to be an inaccurate, unfair evaluation process.

The Learning Loop

Ideally, performance appraisal as a developmental tool provides feedback and the opportunity to discuss present performance. It identifies problems and provides a forum for resolving them, and serves as a basis for the creation of a plan that lets people grow and systematically take on greater responsibility. In practice, performance appraisal, when used in place of a developmental tool, tends to inhibit learning and slow development by inserting an administrative procedure between the individual and his or her performance results, thereby contaminating the information feedback loop.

The learning loop is that phase of the continuous improvement process where information about present performance is provided to individuals and groups so that they can learn and improve. The fact that feedback is fundamental to rapid improvement and organizational learning is irrefutable. Timely feedback is as important to the employee striving to meet his or her goals as it is to the missile whose course must be altered in flight as revised target data are received. Therefore, when feedback to the employee is delayed, filtered, or otherwise perverted, improvement slows and learning suffers.

In many organizations, supervisors are responsible for measuring performance. Feedback from the process goes first to the supervisor who then decides what aspects of the data will be communicated to the worker and how that data will be presented. This introduces a number of significant variables and impediments into the feedback process, including the supervisor's interpretation of the data and the amount of time that elapses between when the data is available and when it is passed on to the worker. Compounding the problem is the fact that, more often than not, the supervisor is also the worker's evaluator, interjecting an element of fear into what should be a learning process.

Another major variable is the supervisor's method of presenting the data. Considered in isolation, data carries no real emotional charge. Introducing another individual into the equation can turn this information transfer into an emotion-charged event, which may thwart rapid and effective learning.

McGregor encouraged managers to devise a better performance management system that didn't undermine an individual's or a team's ability or willingness to learn, but that facilitated more learning. For example, instead of basing performance appraisal primarily on past performance data, wouldn't it make more sense to base the appraisal on what the individual does with that performance information—how he or she uses it to become more productive and improve the process? With this type of appraisal, a person's willingness and ability to think and effectively react to information in real time is what is measured. In such a system, a person's ability to use information wisely becomes more important than short-term performance data. Getting a better report card takes a back seat to learning.

The employee-management communication system at Lincoln puts all parties in constant problem-solving modes. The high level of trust that exists among employees and management allows disagreements to surface in a candid manner. Commitment and trust create the motivation to solve problems in the best interest of the company as a whole.

In a knowledge-based world, better thinking, more effective decision making, and an understanding of reality are critical. It makes little sense, therefore, to interfere with employees trying to achieve these goals by contaminating the information they need to learn, and by evaluating short-term results that are often more attributable to the process itself than to the individual.

Here are 10 guidelines for creating a better performance management system:

1. Determine whether you intend the system to be evaluative or developmental. It's extremely difficult to have both. If you don't

decide, you'll usually end up with a little of both, like it or not. Compromise systems usually don't do either job effectively and often create many negative unintended effects that inhibit our efforts to become more productive.

2. Reduce any *perceived* threats in the system. Face it; if information contained in an appraisal is in any way critical of performance or illuminates mistakes or variations to a boss or supervisor, it is threatening. If people feel threatened, they will act accordingly.

3. Develop self-control—get feedback to the person who will use it first. One way to reduce fear in the appraisal process is to give the person being evaluated the chance to deal with the data before giving it to the boss. Then, have the boss see the data in the context of the employee's analysis.

4. Ensure that everyone can win. Avoid any practice that will limit the number of people who feel they are succeeding. Being rated a 3 (out of 5) rarely feels good. This is especially true if the person being evaluated knows that there isn't a significant difference between his or her performance and others who were graded higher. Putting a behavioral indicator in front of the 3 such as "fully meets expectations" doesn't help. Although conferring these ratings provides organizations with a sense of administrative certainty, most leaders will soon realize how damaging these practices can be to employee morale and performance. If you doubt this is the case, make a list of the advantages and disadvantages of limiting the number of wins in your organization. Your careful analysis, we're convinced, will bear out our point.

5. Eliminate explicit or implicit forced distribution. Who is smart enough to decide ahead of time how many people will perform at a given level? In small groups in particular, why do we persist in advocating the idea of normal distribution? After all, we try to hire the best and we rely on the performance of the critical mass. So, why have a system that alienates the many to reward the few? One unfortunate answer might be to divide people into categories to accommodate the compensation system. Keep in mind, though, that the only thing worse than not getting a raise is not getting a raise and getting a lousy evaluation.

6. Avoid unnecessary or meaningless distinctions. Don't distinguish among performance where no real distinction can be made. Any time you attempt to artificially categorize performance, trust is diminished and the perception of unfairness permeates the system. Forcing people into structured categories often says more about an organization's expectations of its leaders than it does about the performance of the employees who are being evaluated (i.e., by asking supervisors to make these meaningless distinctions, aren't we really implying that they won't confront poor performance unless we force them to)?

7. Evaluate people on their willingness and demonstrated ability to learn. Evaluating short-term process results can inhibit learning and is often more an indicator of the effectiveness (or ineffectiveness) of the process than of individual performance. A far better measure of performance is how well an individual applies his or her learning to better the process. The key to improvement—of one's own performance or of the larger process—is learning. As in any endeavor, if you concentrate on consistently improving your performance, the score will take care of itself. It's amazing how many people know their score, but don't have the discipline, tools, time, or information to systematically improve.

8. Give each person the responsibility for demonstrating the value that they create for the organization. Shouldn't all employees understand specifically what the company has invested in them? Ask each employee to demonstrate how they have added value to the organization and to show how this translates to a return on that investment (for example, through process improvement, product delivery, customer loyalty, innovating product and distribution systems, or increasing the knowledge base of the company). Then use this information to create a dialogue about priorities for the coming months and years. This is a good start toward creating a developmental performance management system that can systematically develop meaningful participation and encourage people to get rid of low or no value-added activities.

9. Every system should require a complete analysis of learnings and areas for improvement. There is always variation to reduce or another hill for the individual to climb. Having people identify these

opportunities can facilitate learning and help reduce fear in the system. When it becomes okay to have shortcomings and when people feel that they can get help in these areas, learning can be significantly accelerated. It seems silly that so many systems recognize the necessity for identifying opportunities for improvement but place that responsibility with the boss. If only the boss knows best, chances are the system is badly broken. If the employee had access to the information that reveals problem areas or, better yet, felt that it was career-enhancing (rather than career-limiting) to point out opportunities for improvement, the ability to learn in the system would be greatly increased.

10. Get rid of any job descriptions that are not redesigned frequently. Why do we use static job descriptions when we desire fast, transformational change, and employees who are constantly learning, innovating new work methods, and taking on new responsibilities? If we must have job descriptions, maybe we ought to track how fast and how often these descriptions change.

Lincoln Electric's performance measurement and reward system provide accurate and timely feedback that helps to encourage learning and build commitment. Lincoln's performance appraisal, compensation, and bonus system increases commitment by equitably distributing the outcomes of production. Employees know they will receive their fair share for the work they do and that the results of their labor will not be distributed disproportionately to top management and to stockholders. This knowledge increases the cooperative attitude of labor toward management and results in enhanced commitment of employees to the organization.

The attitudes of the company toward employee development, encouraging employees to use their full talents in the workplace enhance commitment of employees to the company. As employees develop, their human capital increases and their self-worth and economic productivity increases.

6

Winning with Teams

We have learned that if we push decision-making down in an organization as far as we possibly can, we tend to get better decisions, people tend to grow and to develop more rapidly, and they are motivated more effectively.
—DOUGLAS McGREGOR, *The Professional Manager*

Whenever we've seen examples of a cooperative culture at work, we have been both impressed and moved. Impressed because the team approach generally seems to work (and far better than we had ever dared assume); and moved because, in the absence of internal competition, everyone's actions appear more noble, team goals are put ahead of individual goals, relationships seem deeper, and mutual trust is evident.

If the situation is right and the price is not too high, people will gladly cooperate. People will behave in ways that are consistent with the teamwork that we so desperately need. While we may be culturally biased toward competition, most of us have an even stronger need to be part of something larger than ourselves.

The concept of working in teams is not new. Teams have been around for thousands of years. Tribal societies were teams of action-oriented individuals working together to accomplish common goals for the greater good. But, somewhere along the way it was the individual, not the team, that became the basic building block of most organizations. In fact, many of our organizations revolve largely around individual accountability, individual compensation, individual roles, and job descriptions, and work groups managed by supervisors responsible for the performance of the individuals that make up these groups.

It's time to question the assumptions that lie at the foundation of these practices. The world is just too complicated and our organizations are too diverse to continue to focus primarily on the individual rather than group expertise, nor can we afford the cost of the internal competition that individualism as practiced in most organizations spawns. We can also ill-afford to continue to act as if functions don't need to cooperate and can be managed as piece parts. Individual and functional isolationism is simply too costly and too slow. The genuine interdependencies that exist in today's organization mitigate against it and our customers will not stand for it. There is little question that the way for most of us to win today is no longer in competitive isolation, but by bringing together the expertise necessary to build value.

Without people acting in concert, little gets done effectively. It takes teams—whether we call them that or not—to see a situation from a number of different perspectives and make informed, well-rounded decisions. Teams are the foundation for learning. It is the dialogue, debate, questioning, and confrontation that occurs within a team that allows people to see the world from differing perspectives. Working in teams can also have positive motivational effects. When team members share a common vision and enjoy regular contact with their co-workers, they generally receive faster, more accurate feedback, have more control over their work environment and enjoy a more varied and interesting job experience. With teams there can also be more opportunity for self-management and effective mentoring without playing to the boss. Unnecessary internal competition is often reduced.

In addition, the complexity of managing teams forces leaders to think and act more systemically. This complexity tends to challenge the thinking of supervisors who must evolve a new set of assumptions and practices to manage effectively. And since team members often take on many of the responsibilities now held by supervisors, fewer may be needed. For example, managing 40 individuals is proving difficult (if not impossible) for many supervisors today. Yet it is entirely conceivable that the same supervisor could effectively manage 96 individuals were they organized into a half-dozen or more teams.

A number of those who have written about teams have used the metaphor of a jazz combo or orchestra. In these examples, individual musicians—many with very different talents and playing different instruments—play "as one." Teamwork is not optional, but a prerequisite to successful performance. They are led by someone who coordinates rather than controls, who points the way but does not define it. The individual musicians not only know how to play, they know how to play *together*. Finally, driving each musician's performance is a vision of a given piece that is shared by others. The result is a group performance that is significantly more satisfactory than the sum of its individual parts.

It's Not Easy

Genuinely embracing teamwork rather than just talking about it won't be easy for any number of reasons—not the least being that we are organizations of individuals and proud of it! We also know comparatively little about how to consistently work in teams in an effective and productive way. We are still in our infancy in the quest for understanding when and how to form teams and how to facilitate the best results.

It's not that management hasn't experimented with teams. From teambuilding retreats to self-directed team experiments, almost every organization has dabbled in ways to capture the benefits of individuals working together toward a common goal. Outside of theory, however, the results of our efforts remain mixed. In many cases, we seem to be trying to work in teams while maintaining those structures that focus on individual performance—without seriously questioning the assumptions and beliefs that created these practices. Often the costs have been significant. Ineffective attempts to utilize teams have resulted in wasted time, lower productivity, and reduced levels of trust in many groups.

Now and in the future, many companies will organize in teams not because it furthers employee involvement, but because it is the most efficient way to customize and deliver value in an era where specialization, speed of delivery, and rapid learning are keys to organizational success. There are no recipes for development and management of effective teams. In the end, every leader will have to choose the method that best fits the unique characteristics of his or her organization, the current business climate, and the team members' personal skills and style. In forming a team, however, it may be useful to keep in mind that successful teams usually have:

- *A shared commitment to clearly defined objectives.* While overall team objectives may be broadly stated, the entire team must have a concise understanding of why the team exists and what its specific goals are.
- *Interdependence as an integral element of team design.* An effective team succeeds or fails as a group, with the success of the team requiring a coordinated effort.
- *A compelling purpose that evokes commitment.* This purpose usually evolves in response to challenges from management, customers, or suppliers. However, the team must also understand the *importance* of this purpose. A combination of shared purpose and specific goals is essential.
- *A methodology that facilitates learning.* Too often, teams underperform or fail because they don't have methods for solving problems, analyzing causation, measuring progress, and sharing information.
- *A combination of the right skills and abilities.* Team members are often selected for their position in the organization or for personal or political reasons. This can be problematic. In assembling a team, consider technical skills, knowledge of specific processes, access to information, ability to sustain relationships, understanding of corporate goals, and so on.

- *Mutual accountability as a core value.* Team members must be willing to hold each other accountable. Accomplishing performance goals must be more important than agreement for agreement's sake.
- *Trust from the outset.* Trust must be assumed initially and deepened over time. If we aren't willing to trust others first, we ourselves will never be trusted.
- *A supportive organizational structure.* For teams to thrive, the company's structure should be modified to reduce internal competition and make it career-enhancing for people to subordinate their personal desires in favor of team goals.
- *The challenge to overstretch the present system.* Challenging the team to stretch for objectives that may or may not be attainable under the current system can be teambuilding, energizing, and highly motivational, provided that failure is not punished.
- *Diversity of thought.* A heterogeneous group, the team can bring diversity to the solution of problems. Teams function most effectively when individual team members contribute their own unique approach to problem solving.
- *Quick starters.* Effective teams set shorter rather than longer deadlines. Initial floundering is inevitable, but too much delay can reduce commitment and any sense of urgency the team feels. We often underestimate what can be accomplished in a short period of time.
- *Clear values and rules of behavior.* Every group or social system needs boundaries to provide order to group efforts. Successful teams start by defining a set of expectations or shared values concerning attendance, distractions, loyalty, honesty, respect, willingness to challenge, information sharing, roles, and so on.
- *Significant time to spend as a team.* Team dialogue is a must. The amount and quality of learning and improvement that occur in a team environment correlate directly with the amount of time team members can spend together. You can never anticipate just when the best learning will take place.

- *Regular, structured, honest feedback.* Structuring the opportunity to dialogue is easy compared to the challenge of ensuring that the group is committed to seeing reality and providing honest feedback.

Management Teams

> *Man's social and ego needs will lead him into inevitably meaningful, organized forms of effort, not into indolence.*
> —DOUGLAS McGREGOR, *The Professional Manager*

Although the characteristics of effective teams seem similar at every level in an organization, management teams are more difficult to form and manage effectively. Management teams usually form because of organizational structure and are usually more interested in protecting self-interest than accomplishing goals. Most problems encountered in management teams are caused at the time of formation. Some common failings include:

1. *All direct reports must be on the team.* This becomes a team looking for an issue! It comes together as a result of historical organizational design, rather than in response to the need for a group to solve pressing problems.
2. *The team's goals are the organization's goals.* This results in goals that are often too broad to be effectively addressed by a team.
3. *Goals of the team members are not aligned.* The talk is of acting as a team but performance is still managed individually. Accountability for team performance is often secondary to a manager's individual goals that relate to performance in a part of the organization.
4. *Systems support competitive behaviors more than cooperation.* Present systems often limit the number of team members who can win—get bonuses, raises, performance appraisal marks, and so on. Internal competition results in diminished levels of trust. People who want to cooperate will hesitate if cooperation is punished.

5. *People are selected by position and not their potential to contribute.*

6. *Status differences lessen the willingness of members to challenge ideas and thinking.*

7. *Everyone must be involved in every decision or people feel left out.* Being a team member can become a symbol of success. Since the team's goals are often the organization's goals, involving everyone in everything is inefficient.

8. *Managing the boss' perception is the primary goal of some managers.*

9. *The illusion of agreement is often the implicit goal of the group or "group-think."* Those who confront others are often considered "non-team players."

10. *Systematic feedback on team effectiveness does not exist.*

Nucor's belief system and management philosophy not only provide all shareholders with its mission, vision, and corporate values, but make clear to all the underlining assumptions about its people.

Nucor's Belief System and Management Philosophy

Mission and Competitive Strategy: To build steel manufacturing facilities economically and to operate them productively.

Nucor's Vision of Cooperation: A company is a community of individuals who come together voluntarily to achieve a mission.

Nucor's Assumptions About Its People:

—Dignity/self-worth—Treating employees fairly and with respect.

—Rationality/creativity—Promotes entrepreneurship and develops managerial ability in production workers.

—Human honesty/morality—Culture of freedom.

—Desire to learn—Climate of openness and empowerment.

- Egalitarian culture—status symbols distinguishing management and production workers are minimal.
- Emphasis on employee development and learning.

—Company growth is pursued in order to provide opportunities for employees to learn, develop, earn, and grow.

- Nurturing, coach/team oriented management style.

—Management actively seeks participation of workers in their areas of expertise.

—"Hands on" management style.

- Servant leadership management style.
- Humility and honesty in management.

—Management sees its role as helping workers to develop and grow.

—Mutual respect and trust between management and production workers.

- Order of values regarding stakeholders.

—Customers, employees, and shareholders.

- Market-based management versus command and control style.

Nucor's Belief System and
Management Philosophy *(Continued)*

—Twenty-one independently operated businesses.

—Few services centralized at corporate headquarters.

—Belief that spontaneous order will produce superior results.

- Emphasis on entrepreneurship and innovation for entire workforce.

—Risk taking and high tolerance for mistakes.

- No union or work rules.

Four principles governing employee relations:

1. Management is obligated to manage Nucor in such a way that employees will have the opportunity to earn according to their productivity.

2. Employees should feel confident that if they do their jobs properly, they will have a job tomorrow.

3. Employees have the right to be treated fairly and must believe that they will be.

4. Employees must have an avenue of appeal when they believe they are being treated unfairly.

Reprinted with the permission of John Wiley & Sons, 2000, *Lasting Value* by Joseph Maciariello.

7

Build Cooperation Instead of Internal Competition

A variety of anthropological research point quite definitely to the conclusion that evolution has been a process not only of competition and survival of the fittest but also one of collaboration, cooperation, and mutual support. As one ascends the evolutionary ladder, altruism, idealism, generosity, admiration, and behavior stemming from emotions, are gradually added to the more primitive emotions of hostility and acquisitiveness.
—DOUGLAS McGREGOR, *The Professional Manager*

Managers talk about their employees as being part of a team but, instead of cooperating in a system that encourages teamwork, these same employees are often pitted against one another to compete and win as individuals. As much as we claim we want cooperation, most of our structures don't reward it, our corporate culture doesn't support it, and our leaders are reluctant to embrace it—though it is often in the best interests of the organization to do so. Our people return from their teambuilding weekends and, within a few days (hours?), they're often back to building their empires at the expense of the other team members and with the hope of a superior (i.e., winning) performance appraisal, higher merit pay, the next promotion, or more job security. To meet today's demands, we need to be pulling together, yet the internal competition endemic to our system is undermining our efforts.

We are not saying that cooperation doesn't exist in most organizations. In fact, cooperation can and often does prevail. People frequently act on their more noble instincts and help one another. It is nothing less than amazing that, given the systemic promotion of competition and the resistance to cooperation, there is as much pulling together as there is. It seems that individuals are genuinely driven to do the "right thing"— contributing to the overall good of the organization—rather than feathering their own nests. But the cards in many organizations are essentially stacked against this instinct. There are simply too many barriers to acting decently and cooperatively. Conversely, too many rewards are offered for acting otherwise. If our structure required teamwork, most people would readily cooperate without a library of teambuilding exercises. The task itself would create a cause to rally around.

The organization whose employees must compete for a limited number of wins or rewards—whether it's membership in the President's Circle or the prize for Employee of the Month—tends to create a scarcity mentality of its own, complete with the same scrambling, the same hoarding, the same subversion of potential values, and the same failure to consider the greater good. The principal difference in the type of scarcity that exists in world markets—shortages of food or medicine, for example—and that which exists in the corporation is that the former is real while the latter is artificially created. Organizational structures such as forced-distribution performance appraisal or programs such as sales and service contests get people to compete against one another—a few people win at the expense of others. Ironically, what is scarce and often bitterly fought for in the corporation (e.g., the boss's praise) is not even necessarily something that has real value in the outside world.

The question is "Why do we limit the number of people who can win?" Are there great payoffs for the distinctions we make? What are the potential downside risks? Here, for starters, are eight of these risks:

1. *Internal competition drives out creativity and innovation.* Individuals competing against one another must be playing the same, or similar, game so that the appropriate comparisons can be made and the winners selected. Spawned by competition, this need for similarity makes it more difficult for the individual competitor to experiment and try new methods. The result can be significantly lower levels of creativity and innovation.

2. *Internal competition inhibits dialogue.* Add the concept of winning and losing to a dialogue and you get a debate. In an internally competitive environment, individuals become less interested in sharing and thinking about new or conflicting information and become more concerned with scoring points or pressing their case, right or wrong. After all, in a competition, winning is the name of the game.

3. *Internal competition impacts relationships negatively.* Though many of us naturally expect the best from people, when we know we are competing—whether for a promotion, to curry favor with the boss, or to get a bonus—it is difficult for us to build trust, work as a team member, or create an honest relationship. This is especially so when wins are limited and our victory is made possible by the failure of others. In any event, competition makes people suspicious of one another and often results in greater anxiety in employees, who constantly feel they have to watch their backs.

4. *Internal competition lowers product and service quality.* As different individuals and different departments compete among

themselves while trying to get products and services out as quickly and profitably as possible, the temptation can be to cut corners, particularly if the problems created in doing so won't come back to haunt the company for years, long after the individuals involved have moved on.

5. *Internal competition destroys focus.* Winning and improvement are very different goals. When the focus is on besting others, we are not necessarily focusing on improving the present system. In fact, there is significant evidence demonstrating that winning can actually result in lower levels of performance. When people compete with a focus on winning, they often take the fastest, most reliable, most predictable route to winning, which is rarely the most effective route to continually improving the method of work.

6. *Internal competitiveness reduces efficiency.* When individuals are less innovative, less creative, less trusting, or more combative, it costs the company in a variety of ways. For example, when people compete with one another, they tend to work independently, often duplicating the efforts of others, solving problems that have already been solved, generating data for projects for which perfectly good data already exist.

7. *Internal competition demotivates the non-winners.* The theory was that, if people competed and the winners were rewarded, they would feel appreciated and all those who didn't win would strive to do so in the future. In most cases, however, it hasn't worked out that way. Far too many ill thought-out and incomplete reward systems have resulted in the selection of "winners" whose performance was not any better, and was sometimes objectively worse, than that of some of the "losers." Predictably, this can be demotivating to those who "lost." Precisely how demotivating is hard to tell because we usually evaluate the motivational effectiveness (or ineffectiveness) of our efforts by tracking the reaction of the winners rather than the non-winners. We simply assume that non-winners are generally satisfied and that they'll try harder next time. In fact, the opposite often occurs. Once people are labeled non-winners or

feel that the deck is stacked against them, they sometimes stop trying altogether—and who can blame them?

8. *Internal competition lessens self-esteem.* When some people lose
(or, at least, are labeled non-winners) in the competition, they
begin to question their ability to succeed in this (and maybe any
other) system. After all, they worked hard, tried their best, and
came up short. Losing is more common than winning because the
system has been designed to make sure that most people don't win.
The long-term effect of constantly coming up short can be significant. Less confident people simply don't learn or experiment as effectively as confident people.

Building Cooperation

The compensation and management systems at both Lincoln Electric
and Nucor Steel demonstrate how the flat organization structure has
been effective in enabling each company to react quickly to changes
in the market. The high levels of autonomy seen among the employees at Lincoln and Nucor encourage new thinking and risk taking
among the teams. In addition, by alleviating work rules, teams are
more comfortable engaging in important problem solving and decision making, once relegated solely to the ranks of upper management.
This latitude allowed these teams to contribute to the company's
ability to be adaptable, flexible, and agile in both its operations and
overall strategic objectives.

Their strong sense of community makes Lincoln's employees open
to each other's problem-solving abilities, and the high-trust environment supports a spirit of collaboration since there are fewer questions
about intentions and no worry about individual agendas. The culture of
collaboration and cooperation is tied to Lincoln's bonus system which
creates strong incentives for employees to act autonomously, innovate,
and adapt to new opportunities and problems.

At Nucor steel, the definition of trust is echoed in the company's belief that a *"company is a community of individuals who come together*

voluntarily to achieve a mission." Trust is demonstrated in this proposition first by the choice of words and then through action:

- "Community" implies a mutually beneficial co-existence.
- "Voluntarily" acknowledges that people are free thinkers who have a choice.
- "Mission" implies cohesive action that has drawn the group to act in concert.

These words reflect an attitude that permeates Nucor. To the degree that commitment exists in an organization, it has become instrumental in aligning individual and organizational goals and serves an important role in attaining those goals.

Both Lincoln and Nucor have compensation, bonus, and savings plans that significantly reward employee loyalty, ownership, and cooperation. These programs are supported by formal management systems ensuring that every manager is tied to the performance and growth of his or her team.

For managers whose organizations lack these formal systems, there are many ways to break the hold that internal competition may have on the organization, for example:

- *Increase the interactions between individuals and groups.* The faceless person in another office performing another function can easily be ignored. It's far harder not to cooperate with people you know, especially if your interaction with them is frequent and you have to cooperate to get the job done.
- *Ensure that everyone has the opportunity to win.* This doesn't mean rewarding non-performers. However, when several people seek the same goal and the number of wins is artificially limited, competition will result. If everyone can win, one person's success doesn't necessitate another's failure.
- *Establish cooperation and respect as core values.* As long as internal cooperation is perceived to be optional and internal competition is

tolerated, little will change. Elevating cooperation to a "care" value will ensure that climbing someone else's back to get ahead will be career-limiting. Take a few minutes to analyze whether cooperation is career-enhancing in your organization. How do you know whether people are cooperating effectively? Do you understand the effects of the structures that promote competition? Do your human resource practices encourage teamwork or individual excellence? What happens to people in the organization who play politics at the expense of others?

- *Recognize teamwork, appreciate cooperation, improve recognition abilities.* The more symbolically, visibly, and frequently we demonstrate appreciation for teamwork and interdepartmental cooperation, the more of it we'll get.

- *Educate everyone about the entire process.* If people understand how their performance affects others, they will be less likely to act in ways that negatively impact others or the company. Most people want to do the right thing and, given a choice, will make a good decision unless it is personally punishing. Providing information about the process enables each person to make an informed choice.

- *Beware of quick rotations.* A focus on short-term results often leads to a less cooperative environment. If a person has only a short time in which to impress the boss or make an impact, the long-term benefits of cooperation can be perceived to be less important. This is especially true if a person will be rotated before he or she experiences the negative effects of non-cooperation. In the fast-paced world in which we compete, most jobs don't last long and quick job rotations are necessarily the rule. In these cases, it's even more important to ensure that internal competition is limited and that accountability for cooperation is significant. If part of everyone's evaluation included an analysis of what a person or group has done to further teamwork, most organizations would be very different. Whom have you helped lately? From whom have you learned? Whom have you taught? What group has influenced your thinking the most? Which people, outside your group, have been the most instrumental in helping you succeed?

- *Involve everyone in at least one cross-functional improvement effort.* Mandating that people must work beyond the boundaries of their own department or functional area will result not only in more talent being applied to complicated process issues, but also in a greater appreciation of how the entire process works to benefit the customer. One of the most important reasons for mandating participation may be symbolic, showing people that cooperation is not optional and that everyone will actively participate. People should also be held accountable for their participation. There's no greater waste of time than to be a mandated team member on a team that accomplishes very little.

- *Consider teams as the primary unit of responsibility.* Design in interdependence. It hardly make sense for several members on the team to be able to win when the team as a whole loses and when the customer is shortchanged. If a task requires teamwork, ensure that teamwork is required of everyone. Make the team responsible and accountable. Beware: Although most organizations have begun to organize in teams, many have been unwilling to abandon the old structure completely, keeping team members accountable as individuals to their former functional departments. The result is usually a group that does not function as a team but as individuals representing an area of expertise, each with veto power over most decisions. Frustration levels tend to be high as people are torn between functional responsibilities and group commitments. If we want teams to act like teams, we must make them cohesive units, with a real task and team accountability. Going halfway can be very costly.

8

Building the Intrinsically Motivating, Actualizing Organization

Far less attention has been paid to intrinsic rewards. There are, I believe, two major reasons. The first is the difficulty in establishing a direct link between these rewards and performance. In short, management cannot control or direct intrinsic rewards. The second reason for management's failure to exploit the possibilities of intrinsic rewards is closely associated with beliefs about the nature of man. . . . Managerial practice appears to reflect at least a tacit belief that motivating people "to work" is a mechanical problem.
—DOUGLAS McGREGOR, *The Professional Manager*

Dealing with living organisms and their inherent complexity is the business of physical scientists who have been taught to take a very systematic approach to learning. In a highly disciplined manner, these scientists create hypotheses and then conduct a series of experiments to test their assumptions. Without a hypothesis to test, it would be impossible to learn systematically from the experiments that are conducted. If these scientists were only practical, action-oriented people who shunned theory and fled abstractions, we would know significantly less about our bodies and the universe. Fortunately, they are not. Instead, they accept complexity, chaos, and uncertainty because they know that this is the key to discovery, growth, and solutions of long-lasting utility and import. Besides, in the ever-evolving world of living organisms, complexity, chaos, and uncertainty are all there is. So, too, in the dynamic McGregorian world of business—though most of the systems on which we depend are predicated on exactly the opposite.

Standing in the way of developing a theory for what motivates people—or any organizational theory, for that matter—is that theory is simply not fashionable. For the past decade, much of the world has been preoccupied with the practices of excellent companies and managers, to the exclusion of theory. If we are to learn from the practices of others—as well as from our own experience—we must be able to articulate our core understanding of what drives those experiences—the theory behind them.

To be successful as managers in an arena rife with complexity, chaos, and uncertainty we must take a page from science and learn to evolve a hypothesis about how people are motivated and then test it rigorously against the practices we implement. In doing so, we must resist the temptation to embrace oversimplified models that fail to account for the complexity of individuals. We must take the time to understand people and, more particularly, the individuals that we work with; and we must build the skills necessary to learn systematically in complex environments.

Learning to Learn

To learn effectively in today's complex business environment, we must face the fact that we don't always have the answer and must be accepting, rather than defensive, when our ideas are challenged. This sounds simple but, in organizational settings, it rarely is. In too many organizations, admitting to not having the answer, especially about things as fundamental as leading people, is simply not career-enhancing. This is one of those tough, soul-searching exercises that McGregor felt was the bedrock of modern management.

This can't-afford-to-fail mentality has, in turn, spawned a host of behaviors that seriously hampered management's ability to learn and to become better leaders. Rather than absorbing new information and finding new solutions to emerging problems, many of us have developed a single script for motivating employees that we apply in as many situations as possible. Frequently, too, we are rewarded for our script as if, in implementing it, we understand its far-reaching consequences—even if we ourselves know we don't. Nevertheless, provided our script continues to be successful, we rarely stop to assess why. There is no theory, no experimentation, to our learning beyond whatever theory went into the creation of the initial script. Indeed, in most cases, learning ostensibly ceased after our first positive experience.

On the other hand, when we fail, we immediately stop to determine what went wrong and why. We test our hypothesis. Still, this is rarely the case because our work environment doesn't tolerate too many ineffective tries. If we had failed more, we probably would have built better learning skills. We would have had to learn the consequences of our actions and to examine them in all their complexity. We would have learned more about leadership and the people we lead. We could not have pretended that we knew when we didn't.

Except in the critical area of unleashing the power of the workforce, most of us have been too successful. We've seen our scripts

work again and again and have inured ourselves to the rigors of learning new and improved ones. We've been held accountable for financial results, mostly short-term, but not the results of our ability to
lead a motivated workforce. And, even when "people measures" have
been used to evaluate our success—as in culture surveys—the numbers have been sufficiently vague or our failures sufficiently difficult to quantify as to make accountability nearly impossible. We
simply have not had to face how little we know about people because
our systems and our own adherence to them haven't held us accountable for it.

If we are serious, then, about leading in a personalized, one-size-fits-
one world, we must become more disciplined in our attempt to learn
what makes our co-workers tick. At the same time, we must become
more disciplined in our attempt to understand the organizational system
in which they tick, and the organizational structures that make them tick
in certain ways. We must embrace the complexity of these issues and become avid learners rather than readers of old scripts. This is far easier said
than done. To be a successful leader in this new world, we not only have
to become students again and learn to learn, we have to continue learning throughout our career.

For most of us, the first step in this process is to develop a systematic approach to learning. Fortunately, the tools for this task already
exist in most companies. Whether it is a five-, seven-, or nine-step
continuous improvement process, a Total Quality methodology, or a
systematic learning approach, most companies have been exposed to
good methods for learning to deal with complex processes for some
time now. Though saddled with a variety of monikers, each of these
tools espouses basically the same methodology for learning:

1. Identify the gap between what is and what should be.
2. Identify the probable cause of the gap.
3. Research possible solutions.
4. Test new actions.

5. Measure the differences.

6. Begin the process again.

These learning tools are almost identical to the scientific method most of us learned in high school, with one critical exception: The scientific method demands a hypothesis, which the scientist tests against using experiments. The theory is then revised as a result of new data. By adding theory to the tools that exist in their organizations, most managers already have the wherewithal to improve the learning at their disposal. That's the good news.

The bad news, as we've already mentioned, is that most managers' penchant for action leads them to these tools but away from developing the hypotheses necessary to make these tools effective learning devices. Instead, most managers charge from method to method, tool to tool, and model to model until they get the results they're looking for. And when they don't, instead of trying to understand why, they frequently blame the tool, the consultant, or, worse, the workforce for the failure of the organization to respond to a given implementation. Rarely, in any event, do they blame their own sometimes incomplete and scatter-shot learning methodology. Rather than taking the time to better articulate and understand their own theories about what creates success and what doesn't—particularly when it comes to leading a motivated work-force—many managers have become preoccupied with learning the practices of other excellent companies.

If, as we said before, we are to learn effectively from our experiences (or the experiences of others), we have to have a theory. Without theory, it is too easy to overdose on anecdotes. Without a good understanding of our theories, it is impossible to understand what is specific to a given situation and what is likely to transfer effectively to a different system. Without a complete understanding of our assumptions, we cannot understand the relevance of the techniques and tools we choose and are all too likely to introduce one program, one initiative after another until the entire workforce is confused or cynical.

argument & consequence — coaching
for   of not

For an organization to operate as a learning organization it must be viewed and analyzed in terms of its being an open system. The shared vision created by this openness is one that *encourages individual learning and team problem solving*, and is continuously seeking new knowledge as a source of motivation and of competitive advantage. We certainly see these attributes at present at both Lincoln and Nucor.

The management style most supportive of the learning organization is a coaching and participative one. Because the rate of change is so great, authoritarian, command and control management systems where corporate executives develop a strategy that is then implemented by the rest of the organization, are not agile enough for the environment. And they never tap the full potential of people at all levels of the organization.

The learning organization requires management systems that encourage developing the talent of all of the people in the organization. Further, the talent of each individual should be applied in a manner that is consistent with the vision of the organization as a whole. People become an organization's most valuable asset in a learning organization and the development of people becomes the most important task of management.

Managers at Nucor serve as mentors who see themselves as working for employees and helping them to become productive and innovative. Supervisors and managers seek to improve the economic condition of employees by helping them become more productive.

The management style at both Lincoln and Nucor reinforces the attributes of performance, development, and learning.

Building an Environment in Which Motivated People Can Contribute

> *New organizations, new institutions will be created by the intensification, by the competition for talent that will no longer be available or attracted by the promise of extrinsic rewards alone.*
>
> —DOUGLAS McGREGOR, *The Professional Manager*

Earlier, we posed McGregor's question, "How do you motivate employees?" We'll return to McGregor for the answer: "You don't. Man is a living organism, not a machine." This belief in the relative unmotivatability of humans because they are living organisms led McGregor to a theory of motivation with which we concur and which informs the later sections of this book.

Stated simply, McGregor's theory is that most people are born motivated to pursue what they perceive they need and that, if we want a motivated workforce, we must build and continually modify an environment in which people can fulfill these needs while pursuing the goals of the organization.

The obvious key to the successful implementation of this theory is alignment of personal needs and organizational goals. Any discussion of motivation must take this concept of alignment into primary consideration. This is particularly true if what we hope to achieve is more than mere compliance. The argument follows that, once this alignment is achieved, businesses can benefit from the natural tendency of employees to act to fulfill their needs and, as they go about doing so, their actions will be consonant with the best interests of the organization. The challenge then, for those who concur with McGregor's theory or derivations of it, lies not in motivating people but in building an environment in which motivated people are willing to make a maximum contribution.

Most discussions of people's needs begin with a basic understanding of the work generally associated with Abraham Maslow. Its central thesis is that human needs are organized in a hierarchy, with needs for survival, food, and shelter at its base. At progressively higher levels in Maslow's hierarchy are needs for security and social interaction, with the highest level being the need to learn, grow, and reach one's potential. According to Maslow, as lower level needs become reasonably well satisfied, successively higher levels become more influential in motivating behavior. Also, when lower levels, such as security, remain unsatisfied, less energy remains for high-level activity, such as learning, creativity, or building self-esteem.

This is not to say that when lower levels are satisfied; they are no longer an issue. On the contrary, Maslow noted that people seem to have an insatiable ability to become dissatisfied with what he referred to as "environmental factors." Even when survival is not in question and people are reasonably well paid, they usually want to be paid better. Also, it's a rare individual who is completely secure in his or her work environment. Today more than ever, that insecurity may be well-founded. As for our social needs, they wax and wane on the strength of our personal relationships and our participation with others in the organization.

Reasonable satisfaction in Maslow's construct does not equate to complete satisfaction. Rather, reasonable satisfaction is achieved when, in the perception of the individuals involved, environmental factors like pay and job security are adequately addressed and equitably administered. People who feel that they are adequately and fairly paid do not spend most of their days thinking about their salary unless other environmental factors lead them to do so. People who feel that their health insurance is basically fair will not be preoccupied with the specific terms of the insurance contract. When discipline is handled consistently, most people are able to manage the risk of failure without allowing that risk to distract them unnecessarily.

Even when the actual amount of pay and benefits is substantial, however, if people feel that they are unfairly administered, the demotivational effect can be substantial. Only when people feel substantially satisfied in terms of both actual need satisfaction and relative fairness, can they begin to focus on finding ways to concentrate their efforts on learning and growth. Alas, many of our present practices have been designed in ways that make relative fairness nearly impossible.

Nucor's success, like Lincoln's, can be attributed to numerous factors but three are especially noteworthy. First and foremost is Nucor's *belief and respect for people* that in turn supports an environment of mutual interdependence and cooperation. Nucor maintains a high view of human potentiality. Management's hypothesis is if you select your personnel carefully and believe that your people are trustworthy, self-starting, self-reliant, hardworking, and motivated, those are the attributes you are likely to find in your workforce. And those are the same attributes that these individuals will seek to actualize through their work.

Building Organizational DNA

> *The manager's role as a manager is enhanced (and complicated) by the fact that he is also a human being who has developed a set of values. He possesses firm, emotionally based beliefs about what is "good" and "bad" with respect to the religious, political, social, economic, and personal aspects of life. He cannot leave these behind when he goes to work. Yet the fact is that there are basic conflicts of this sort that appear to be almost impossible to resolve. Will he marry the job if this involves shirking his responsibilities as a husband and father? Will he become a "servant of the corporation" and rationalize or ignore his own personal values when they conflict with the impersonal, efficiency-dominated profit maximization oriented values of the economic enterprise? Will he accept and support decisions and policies made by others which, at least occasionally, are in conflict with his conceptions of fair and just treatment of fellow human beings?*
> —DOUGLAS McGREGOR, *The Professional Manager*

It is currently fashionable and appropriately so, to compare the organization to a huge and highly complex self-organizing physical system or organism. Looking at such a system under a microscope, we would see a stable center. Yet, at its periphery, where it encounters the external environment, the system appears chaotic. Keeping the organism intact and functional in the face of this chaos is the DNA molecule that is carried by virtually every cell in the system. Each of these molecules, in turn, contains a genetic fingerprint of the larger organism of which it is a part. Cells found in an animal's hair or blood, for example, share the same unique DNA pattern as those that make up its bones or skin. Every cell will always be characteristic of that system—even as old cells die and new ones take their place—they will assume the same shape, organization, and behavior.

Applied to the organization, there is a systemic code of information—organizational DNA—carried by every employee as well as a link to the organization's stable core—its vision, values, and decision-making criteria. In organizations where this code exists, individuals—even those thousands of miles from headquarters and thousands of miles from one another—all function as members of that system. Therefore, when confronted with similar problems or requests, they will tend to make similar decisions. In other words, the organization can support decentralized decision making, maintaining a sense of order even as it adapts to a changing environment.

Unfortunately, many of today's organizations don't have this organizational DNA, either because there is no shared vision, because values aren't articulated (and lived), because decision-making criteria have not been established, or a combination of the three. In its place, most organizations have extensive rules that have proliferated to accommodate every possible situation. We've all seen the countless manuals and SOPs that govern every action and inform every decision made in the organization. We've also seen how referring to these manuals—in actual fact or in our heads—often slows the process and gets in the way of delighting customers. Aware of how counterproductive rules can be, some of us have significantly reduced their number. In place of the rules, we've empowered people to act—only to find that they are reluctant to assume that responsibility because, in the absence of organizational DNA, the risk of doing so is simply too great.

How can we go about creating organizational DNA in our organization? How can we genetically engineer this essential substance to enable us to decentralize our decision-making process and give people the parameters they need to act along with the power we may have already given them? Not, we're convinced, by looking to the Disneys and Nordstroms of the world, companies whose DNA has been forged through decades of experience and handed down through generations of employees. Trying to copy the methods of a Disney or Nordstrom without their history and pervasive cultures will quickly prove frustrating for most companies—although these organizations and others like them can serve as long-term models.

In today's world, we need people willing to take risks to improve the process and better serve the customer. Without DNA coursing through the organization, there's no effective way to manage risks, so people will simply shy away from taking them. With DNA, we can all take risks, we can all fail, and we can all learn. And we can do it knowing that we will be supported, without the fear of being branded a failure.

Toward a New Theory of Motivation

> *To a considerable degree, man has been*
> *perceived to be like a physical body at rest.*
> *The application of external force is required to*
> *set him in motion—to motivate him to work.*
> *Consequently, extrinsic rewards and*
> *punishment are the obvious and appropriate*
> *forces to be utilized in controlling human*
> *effort. Nothing could be further from the truth.*
> —DOUGLAS McGREGOR, *The Professional Manager*

In his classic *Harvard Business Review* article first published in 1957, "An Uneasy Look at Performance Appraisal," McGregor consistently commented on the importance of an individual's willingness to give the job his all and the role of the manager to spark that enthusiasm. It was clear to McGregor (as well as his contemporaries and protégés) that the "carrot-and-stick" philosophy of motivation where managers dangled a deeply desired item in front of the employee in the hope of inspiring some type of work ethic was not effective in building long-term loyalty, trust, and performance. What McGregor insightfully suggested was that extrinsic motivation was not enough. When a person is said to be extrinsically motivated, that person is seeking a reward or avoiding a punishment that is external to the activity itself.

Many of us have significant experience in using extrinsic rewards and punishments to influence behavior. Employee of the Month, Man of the Year, management incentive plans, pay-for-performance schemes, and performance appraisal-linked promotion and pay are some examples. Much of our early training had behavior modification—that is, rewards—as its basic tenet. We learned if we reward positive behavior, its repetition is more likely; ignoring a behavior tends to discourage it; and punishing a behavior will probably suppress it.

Hungry people might be easier to control because they cannot afford not to comply. In their minds, it is often perceived to be more important to keep their jobs or get promoted than it is to do the right thing in pursuit of a mutually held objective. For too long, many have confused compliance with commitment—and compliance breeds resentment.

Extrinsic Rewards

- *Can change the way people approach their work.* If the proposition is "Do this and you'll get that," people will often focus more on the "that," the reward, and less on the "this," the job. In an extrinsic environment, the task can become secondary to the attainment of the reward. Perhaps the most profound and farthest-reaching fallout that can result from the use of extrinsic rewards is a reduction in a worker's commitment to his or her work. If this is true—and study

Extrinsic Rewards *(Continued)*

after study indicates it is—then rewards are not just innocuous incentives that may or may not entice employees. Rather, rewards can actually promote or heighten disinterest and resentment in the job to be done. Or, as author Alfie Kohn says, "The more you want what was dangled in front of you, the more you may come to dislike whatever you have to do to get it."

- *Can be perceived to be controlling and manipulative.* Generally, extrinsic rewards put the rewarder in a position of power and control over the rewardee—or at least reinforce that power and control, with most rewards being like gifts with strings attached. Sure, you want the present, but the conditions attached often left a bad taste in your mouth. You knew you were being manipulated, just like workers know they are being manipulated by rewards on the job, and many don't like it. Rewards also tend to color whatever personal relationship exists between the rewarder and the rewardee.

- *Can discourage creativity.* Though initial logic suggests otherwise, rewards actually cut down on the inclination to be flexible or innovative. People working for rewards usually seek the most predictable solution that will afford them a payoff as quickly as possible, with the least chance of failure. Given the choice between striking out in new directions or using past solutions that have worked, the reward seeker will probably opt for the latter.

- *Don't lead to lasting change.* If you are trying to change behavior, extrinsic rewards can work over the short term. To sustain any behavioral change over the long term, you have to keep giving rewards, and in most cases increase the ante as time

(continued)

Extrinsic Rewards *(Continued)*

goes on. As for changes in attitude or interest levels, rewards usually have little positive effect on either.

- *Encourage inappropriate solutions to complex problems.* For example, if salespeople are not featuring a particular product in their sales efforts, providing a reward for them to do so may distract you from an essential problem with the product or, worse yet, may entice the salesforce to find a way to sell a product to a customer who doesn't need it.
- *Impede the leader's development of leadership skills.* Paying or otherwise rewarding a person to do his or her job differently is much easier than building the leadership skills necessary to engage in the kind of serious give and take required to build a shared commitment for change.
- *Are expensive.* In a world of shrinking financial resources, it would seem that dangling rewards—usually in the form of bonuses or merit pay—in front of employees is contrary to the direction most organizations are seeking to take. In addition, today's rewards will not be adequate tomorrow. For rewards to continue working, they must continue to spiral upward in value. The more that rewards are used, the more they are needed.
- *Can be punishing.* The effectiveness of many reward programs is evaluated by assessing the subsequent performance of those who are rewarded. But what about those who do not get the rewards? Often rewards are given to people whose performances are not substantially different from those who were not rewarded. In other cases, failures in our information systems have resulted in rewards being given to people who are *less* deserving than their peers. The de-motivational effects on the many who go unrewarded frequently outweigh the motivational effects on the few who got the prize.

Commitment is a personal choice. If people do not feel that they can make the choice because they cannot afford to live with the repercussions, there is no real choice and, therefore, no commitment. Perceived security is a prerequisite to building commitment. And we were consistently taught that our job as managers was to ensure that specific rewards were linked, by those we managed, to specific organizational goals. Ironically, these ingrained teachings about behavior modification—about the use of extrinsic rewards and punishments to get people to do what we want them to do—may be the biggest stumbling blocks to building a workforce committed to the job and not the reward that comes after.

Forget the Carrot!

> It is often argued that most people are by
> nature dependent—that they prefer not to
> accept responsibility but to be led. If we
> observe their behavior on the job, the
> generalization appears to hold rather widely.
> Yet it is surprising that these same people not
> only accept responsibility but seek
> responsibility in a variety of organized
> activities away from the job.
> —DOUGLAS McGREGOR, *The Professional Manager*

Intrinsic rewards, on the other hand, are inherent not in the reward but in the activity itself—that is, the reward is in the achievement of the goal. Intrinsic rewards cannot be directly controlled externally although the characteristics of the environment in which the individual functions can enhance (or limit) his or her opportunity to obtain these rewards. Achievements of knowledge, skill, or autonomy; self-confidence and respect; the exhilaration that comes from personal growth; the satisfaction that comes from helping others or being socially responsible are examples of intrinsic rewards.

For a variety of reasons, most of us have learned far less about, and paid less attention to, intrinsic rewards. The primary reason for this lies with our need to be able to measure the results of our interventions. It is often difficult to establish a direct link between the leader's creation of an intrinsically motivating environment and the enhanced ability of followers to thrive, grow, and better serve customers in that environment. The causal connection between a manager offering a reward for achieving sales goals and a salesperson working overtime to win that reward seems obvious to both the offerer and the recipient. It is virtually impossible, however, to demonstrate the causal relationship of a salutary work environment to an individual's or group's increased sense of self-worth gained from implementing an improvement that is fundamental to the success of the organization.

As managers in an intrinsically rewarding environment, we can also lavish praise on employees, but no one but employees themselves can provide the reward that counts the most: a genuine sense of accomplishment. Most of us like to know the result of our leadership interventions and, without direct feedback, we can never be sure of the effects of our actions. We like the certainty of knowing, and we often avoid that which cannot be directly proven. We like to be in control, and we can't control intrinsic satisfaction beyond creating and controlling the environment in which it takes place.

A second reason that some managers have failed to experiment adequately with an intrinsically motivating environment may be negative assumptions they hold about people and their work ethic: If managers don't believe that employees are capable of finding work interesting and exciting, they won't experiment with different environments. In today's relatively enlightened work environment, most managers would resist saying outright that they don't believe people are capable of learning and growing on the job. The fact is that many managers are quick to identify certain members of their organization as people who actively seek responsibility and are capable of accepting more of it. But, often, these same managers are just as quick to note that far more people in the organization can't be trusted to simply want to get the maximum reward with a minimum of effort. Therefore, many managers note, given the present makeup of the workforce, creating an intrinsically motivating environment (one less reliant on the manipulation of extrinsic rewards) is impractical. With so few rewards in the work itself for most employees, these managers conclude, the only practical solution is to continue to depend on extrinsic rewards. In this way, employee behavior can be controlled. At least, compliance can be achieved, even if it means forgoing commitment.

What makes the extrinsic conclusion far too seductive for many managers is that they feel more comfortable thinking in terms of meting out cheese to rats in a maze as a reward for desired behavior than reshaping their thinking or rewriting their script. It's easy, it's surefire, and it's relatively safe. With enough power, we can even predict people's reactions with some certainty. We can organize specifically for desired tasks. Extrinsic incentives fit our tendency to view the behavior of the workforce in mechanical terms. Relying primarily on extrinsic rewards and punishments reduces our risk, and it enables us to get short-term results without having to adjust the environment in ways that would challenge our assumptions. It's simple, and we like simple. And because in years past, the competitive environment did not require a maximum contribution from people, we survived. That was yesterday, however. Tomorrow promises to be different.

There must be a better way for us to exercise our leadership skills than meting out cheese. People are not rats in a maze; they are capable of great achievements. We have all had experiences where people were challenged to do the outrageous and have exceeded everyone's expectations. Why don't we think that that is possible day in and day out in our organizations? Why do we settle for so much less?

The Dark Side of Incentives

The problem with most extrinsic incentives is not only that they undermine employee commitment through their focus on rewards rather than work, but that they actually interfere with creating the highly flexible learning environment that we all need if we are to succeed in a self-actualizing world. Consider what happens when we use extrinsic incentives to modify people's behavior; the promise of money if certain goals are achieved, for example. Unless they are independently wealthy, most people will not only take the fastest, most direct route to the money but will often resent what they have to do to get it. By holding out the promise of money—and the threat of not getting it—employees are forced to scramble for it any way they can, often at the price of doing the best job possible. At the same time, harking back to Maslow, this threat to survival and security drops the individual down the hierarchy of needs and robs him or her of the energy necessary to focus on the learning and creativity required to satisfy today's demanding workplace.

This same dynamic comes into play with traditional performance appraisal. If I become worried that my appraisal may affect my promotion and, therefore, my family's ability to maintain its quality of life, I am again forced down Maslow's hierarchy from the highest level, where I do my best work, to a lower level, where I spend much of my energy helping to ensure my survival and security.

Internal competition for extrinsic rewards can have a similar effect, particularly when the competition clearly defines winners and losers. We have seen high-level executives expend considerable time and energy competing with their peers for bonuses, perks, and status within the organization, often doing things that they knew were not in the best interests of their stakeholders. No one wants to be a loser in the eyes of his or her peers. People want to succeed; a loss knocks them down a level on Maslow's hierarchy, providing them with less time and energy to devote to higher level achievements.

Here, as in the other examples we have cited, "losing" an individual's creativity in the service of the company and the customer is compromised in the name of management's attempt to control behavior through extrinsic rewards. Given the demands of a McGregorian world, we believe that forcing employees down Maslow's hierarchy and compromising employee creativity is simply too high a price to pay for control. Besides, frequently the control that these extrinsic rewards promise—particularly when coupled with close supervision and/or the machine-assisted mon- itoring that has recently become popular—is illusory. People can and do resist control, and these tactics will often provoke a feeling of loss of personal freedom among employees. At that point, the impulse is to re- sist control, not give into it, leading to an unproductive and expensive cycle of ever-greater manipulation and control, and increasing resist- ance to it.

We have to make a choice: whether to continue to keep a close rein on the workforce in an environment that promises compliance at best or whether to create a new, intrinsically motivated environment where the work itself provides its own rewards and where people can fulfill their own needs while committing themselves to the organization's objectives.

Lincoln's management systems are full of devices that build commit- ment through a system of intrinsic rewards that begins as early as when the employee is recruited. In recruiting production workers, Lincoln se- lects one in 75 applicants. Clearly, the company is seeking highly moti- vated people who bring with them the strong desire to succeed. Another aspect of Lincoln's management system that promotes employee commitment and gives employees a sense of permanence is the promise of continuous employment after a probationary period. This is rein- forced by widespread employee ownership of company stock through various stock purchase and 401k plans. Employee ownership of shares in Lincoln provides them with a long-term personal interest in the eco- nomic welfare of the company. Participation supports commitment and self-actualization, and Lincoln's employees are completely involved in decisions which affect their work. Lincoln's advisory board is crucial here, but so are all of the other informal arrangements such as nonbu- reaucratic behavior, management by walking around and the open door policy of top executives.

Testing Your Assumptions

Are we ready and willing to face the following realities? The problem with the workforce is not that they don't respond to motivation but with the methodology we have used to try to motivate them; that people are behaving much as we have asked them to; that their reactions to our manipulation of rewards and punishments are predictable; and that these same people, given the right environment, the right tools, and the autonomy to be successful, are capable of making great strides in finding new and creative ways to build relationships with our customers.

If we are willing, then we need to begin our journey by identifying those behaviors and systems that people in the organization perceive to be inequitable and we need to destroy them—even before we have a tried-and-true replacement. We need to formulate a theory that describes the type of environment in which people can learn, grow, and make a contribution. We must learn from our experiments and resist the temptation to resort to carrot-and-stick mentality of rewards the next time things don't go perfectly. We must also accept that we won't do everything right the first time or even the second, but by persisting, we will learn and get better with every try.

Fortunately, accompanying us on this challenging journey will be the individuals who serve our customers, employees motivated to make a valuable contribution, men and women eager to do the best job they can. And it is our job as leaders and guides on this odyssey to provide them with that opportunity.

Creating the Intrinsically Motivating, Value-Driven Workplace

> *Management must seek to create conditions*
> *(and an organizational environment) so that*
> *members of the organization at all levels can*
> *best achieve their own goals by directing their*
> *efforts toward the goals of the organization.*
> —DOUGLAS McGREGOR, *The Professional Manager*

In theory, empowerment is about the redistribution of authority and accountability in the organization. Most often it takes the form of

Herman Miller: McGregor in Action

Founded in 1923 by D.J. DePree, Herman Miller, Inc. (Zeeland, MI) is one of the world's leading manufacturers of commercial office furniture and a provider of furniture management services. The company uses both formal and informal management systems to promote employee-owner values, participative management, and environmental responsibility.

Known for its space-age furniture designs and progressive management system, Herman Miller rigorously considers the input of its employee-owners whose high level of commitment is supported by the spirit of corporate community instilled into the company's organizational design and structure.

While Herman Miller readily changes its business practices to fit an ever-evolving marketplace, their belief and value systems remain steadfast. These qualities are again infused throughout the company's processes and policies. The company is committed to cultivating community participation and people development. It believes in aligning individual goals with those of the organization, and values community because of the strength and power that comes from uniting thousands of individuals, with truly diverse perspectives, opinions, skills, and backgrounds in a common purpose. Herman Miller's corporate community is comprised of all of the company's stakeholders: suppliers, dealers, customers, designers, and other partners. Through diversity, united in a common purpose, Herman Miller remains a creative and flexible organization that adjusts rapidly to market changes. The community is built on competence and performance and has at its core participation and employee development.

Management's belief in the accountability of the entire workforce is evident in the amount of autonomy given to employees

(continued)

Herman Miller: McGregor in Action *(Continued)*

and the company's emphasis on their workforce as employee-owners. The idea of employee-owners is a message consistently repeated throughout all of Herman Miller's policies, practices, and public statements. Living with integrity and respecting the environment are also attributes that are reinforced through the company's formal and informal practices.

Herman Miller is an organization that personifies those qualities McGregor attributed to the intrinsically-rewarding workplace, where higher human ideals are forged to create a seamless organization who's goals, motivations, and actions are all geared toward a shared purpose.

---

granting greater decision-making power to front-line employees to enable them to improve the way work is done or to customize the process for customers.

In most implementations, however, companies attempting to empower employees still retain their traditional organizational structure, where power emanates from the top. This can result in confusion: the front-line worker has supposedly been empowered, yet the old system dictates that power be held at higher levels and that managers be held accountable for the front-line worker's actions. For the front-line worker, this semi-delegation of authority can be little more than an organizational tease since the true power remains with the manager and all that is actually redistributed is some of the manager's responsibility. Often, empowered workers are not given the background and training necessary to successfully carry out their new responsibilities.

Also hampering these efforts is that the power granted to employees is usually conferred on a provisional basis. Since in most implementations managers remain in control and are ultimately responsible, they can revoke authority whenever they deem that employees are not using it wisely. This patriarchal aspect of empowerment frequently results in employees who feel that they are not genuinely trusted.

In most instances, empowerment is an attempt to bring about a new result while still working from an old set of assumptions. These assumptions, as we've said elsewhere in this book, view labor primarily as an instrument of production. In the industrial world where production was king and the role of employees and managers simple and clear-cut, these assumptions held a definite appeal. They kept production costs down, fed the need for mass production, and kept investments in training at a minimum. But what could their appeal be today, when distribution and delivery of products and services to a loyal customer base by a loyal workforce are key to survival? How do these old assumptions square with management's oft-stated goal of having employees treat the company's money as if it were their own?

If our goal is to get people to act like owners—to treat the company's money like their own, to treat the company's customers like their own, and to commit to their work as an owner might—then it's time to move beyond what we have come to know as empowerment and create a true sense of "ownership" through formalized structures that go deep into the design of the organization.

In engendering a sense of ownership in employees, it may be helpful to think of them as independent contractors or business owners whom we've hired to produce value for the company. What is the value we expect of them? How much is it worth to us? How will we determine whether we receive the expected or greater value? Thinking of employees in these terms allows us to consider their value and importance to the company in a new light and forces us to determine whether the tasks they perform are genuinely necessary and/or valuable.

By that same token, if employees are urged to see themselves as independent contractors with a generally-defined role in the process, they will take greater responsibility for creating the value their "organization" has been asked to deliver. This may take the form of helping develop or improve the process, anticipating changes in customer needs and requirements, solving problems, improving productivity, and ensuring a good return on the investment that is being made in them. Although these employees may not have legal ownership of the company's assets, they will in fact own something that may be even more significant: They will own the responsibility for making a meaningful contribution.

The organizational landscape is full of companies whose employees own stock but who don't feel (or act) like owners. That's because a sense of ownership only comes when we are convinced that our contribution is a meaningful one—when we are committed to the work we do, the customers we serve, and the teammates we work with. While stock ownership may involve us financially, it does little to involve us emotionally.

The Rewards of Being McGregorian

Herman Miller Corporate Awards

- 1999: Herman Miller maintains its consistent ranking (since 1986) as *Fortune* magazine's "Most Admired" furniture manufacturer in America, with the company's reputation scoring thirteenth among all American industry, and third among all companies for both Innovation and Social Responsibility.
- 1999: *Forbes* magazine's inaugural "Platinum List" of America's 400 best-managed, large companies.
- 1999: *Fortune* magazine again cites Herman Miller among the "100 Best Companies to Work for in America."
- 1998: Council for Economic Priorities (CEP) first annual Honor Roll Awards for a consistent record of social and environmental leadership.
- 1998: *Fortune* magazine noted Herman Miller as the "Most Admired" company in America for Social Responsibility.
- 1998: *Fortune* magazine recognized Herman Miller among the "100 Best Companies to Work for in America."
- 1997: Max DePree and Herman Miller recognized by the Business Enterprise Trust for "sound management and social vision."
- 1993: Herman Miller named one of four winners nationwide of the Beacon Award—for excellence in integrated corporate communications and design programs—sponsored by *Fortune* magazine and the American Center for Design.
- 1992: Max DePree, chairman of the board, named to *Fortune* magazine's Hall of Fame.
- 1991: Business and Aging Leadership Award from the United States Administration on Aging for exceptional leadership in the development of innovative policies and programs.
- 1990: D.J. DePree, founder, inducted into the American Business Hall of Fame.

9

Creating a Cause Worthy of Commitment

Human beings aspire to be a part of a cause worthy of commitment.
—DOUGLAS McGREGOR, *The Professional Manager*

One of the keys to winning employee commitment is to create a cause that is worthy of such commitment. It is also critical that we provide the opportunity for learning and that we design processes that people can control to create value instead of processes that control people. A mindset that results in employees being systematically denied training and information flies in the face of our pronounced need for the well-trained, well-informed worker. Indeed, in today's competitive, information-sensitive world, we'll have to continuously retrain experienced workers for more complex tasks. Undertrained employees will not be able to reliably analyze information and make the real-time decisions that will be required. Uninformed, partially committed employees cannot be expected to effectively innovate, deliver, or ensure customer loyalty. On the other hand, if our organizations provide employees with a worthy cause, interesting work, sufficient training, and the opportunity to reach their potential, the chances are excellent that they will make the commitment we seek.

Unfortunately, most jobs have not been designed to produce value for the customer while also providing an opportunity for the development of the employee. In fact, in a large percentage of cases, just the opposite is true. We've designed jobs and written job descriptions in ways that make sense from an efficiency standpoint, but that do little to feed the needs of people to learn, grow, and be challenged. In the short run (quarter to quarter), the current system may even seem effective. However, as the organization increasingly calls on the intelligence of its people to build new capabilities, the price we're paying for these "efficiencies" is already too steep.

Is it possible to create an interesting, challenging job for every employee? Can we really organize so that every employee has a chance to grow and prosper? And, more to the point, is it even possible to accomplish this without turning the organization completely on end? The answer is yes—provided that we make the change from the old-fashioned, factory-based, production-oriented mindset to one that better accommodates flexibility and responsiveness and, above all, expects significant contributions from everyone in the company in both the planning and execution of their jobs.

Certainly, not all jobs are equally interesting, nor can every job be made to seem appealing. This is particularly true in inherently unchallenging, highly-repetitive, low-paying, little-experience required jobs, of which there are millions. However, in most of these jobs, interest and commitment are possible for many employees if, in addition to the performance of the task, they are charged with the management of the process.

What would this entail? Eight responsibilities are at the foundation of process improvement efforts:

1. *Gather information.* In the normal course of business, employees should regularly seek feedback from customers, suppliers, and part-

ners about what they like or don't like about the company's products and services and what they'd like to see done differently. This data should be quickly analyzed by those collecting it and then be communicated throughout the organization.

2. *Help design the service delivery process.* Being involved in this design must be predicated on an understanding of the entire delivery process, not just the job that the employee performs. Everyone must have a substantial understanding of the implications of their work and have the ability to influence the design of the way that work is accomplished.

3. *Customize the process when necessary.* Why is it that some employees don't act in the customer's best interest when common sense often dictates a different, obvious course of action? Often, it's because many workers still aren't trusted to make even the simplest deviations in the process and must get supervisory approval to do so. For an organization to be considered responsive in the future, this must change.

4. *Measure the quality of their own performance.* The primary benefit to be gained from measuring your own performance is that the direct, unfiltered feedback you receive when doing so enhances learning. Whether you are or aren't allowed to measure your own performance is often an issue of trust. Many managers believe that workers are unable (haven't been trained) to measure their performance effectively and won't identify areas where they have weaknesses (too much risk). Wouldn't they be more honest in their self-appraisal if fear were eliminated from the process?

5. *Identify disgruntled customers.* Often, the customers we lose are the ones who are marginally dissatisfied but are not particularly vocal about it. Most customers don't complain; they just move on. Customer-contact employees can often head off such losses if they are given the responsibility to seek out those quiet, unhappy customers and do something to alleviate the causes of dissatisfaction quickly.

6. *Find the root cause of service problems.* In most service companies, management controls the process, and only a few groups have been

trained to analyze information effectively to determine the root cause of problems. Rectifying this shortcoming will require education and time. Many companies still claim that they can't "afford" to give employees time to meet for an hour or two at the end of every week to discuss what they learned that week and to set priorities for improvements in the coming week. To be successful in the future, they can't afford not to.

7. *Improve the process.* Innovation and continuous improvement of processes have not traditionally been responsibilities of most employees. There is a significant difference between performing a task and playing a part in managing a process. The former can get repetitive quickly; the latter is continually engaging.

8. *Have the power to routinely eliminate nonvalue-adding tasks.* In most organizations, many people are involved in some unproductive activities. Typically, only managers can choose to eliminate these value-subtracting tasks. Why? If we respect people's minds, why don't we trust them to get rid of activities that waste their time—or at least build a process that enables them to point out wasteful activities without fear of retaliation?

Focusing on Involvement and Accountability

In many companies, the attempt to increase employee involvement has been more fad than passion. In the abstract, employee involvement seemed like a good idea. But when it came right down to it, redefining jobs to make them more challenging and giving employees greater responsibility was either too daunting, too hard, or too threatening and disruptive for managers. The shape of tomorrow's successful organizations is becoming clear, however. Although many companies have survived failed attempts at greater employee involvement in the past, it seems unlikely that they will be so lucky in the future.

The road to creating an organization in which employees can take responsibility for making a meaningful contribution will not be an easy

Worthington Industries' Philosophy

Earnings: The first corporate goal for Worthington Industries is to earn money for its shareholders and increase the value of their investment. Worthington believes that the best measurement of the accomplishment of our goal is consistent growth in earnings per share.

Our Golden Rule: We treat our customers, employees, investors, and suppliers, as we would like to be treated.

People: We are dedicated to the belief that people are our most important asset. We believe people respond to recognition, opportunity to grow, and fair compensation. We believe that compensation should be directly related to job performance and therefore use incentives, profit sharing or otherwise, in every possible situation. From employees we expect an honest day's work for an honest day's pay. We believe in the philosophy of continued employment for all Worthington people. In filling job openings, every effort is expended to find candidates within Worthington, its divisions, or subsidiaries. When employees are requested to relocate from one operation to another, it is accomplished without financial loss to the individual.

Customer: Without the customer and his need for our products and services, we have nothing. We will exert every effort to see that the customer's quality and service requirements are met. Once a commitment is made to a customer, every effort is made to fulfill that obligation.

Suppliers: We cannot operate profitably without those who supply the quality raw materials we need for our products. From a pricing standpoint, we ask only that suppliers be competitive in the marketplace and treat us as they do their other customers. We are loyal

(continued)

Worthington Industries' Philosophy *(Continued)*

to suppliers who meet our quality and service requirements through all market situations.

Organization: We believe in a divisionalized organizational structure with responsibility for performance resting with the head of each operation. All managers are given the operating latitude and authority to accomplish their responsibilities within our corporate goals and objectives. In keeping with this philosophy, we do not create corporate procedures. If procedures are necessary within a particular company operation, that manager creates them. We believe in a small corporate staff and support group to service the needs of our shareholders and operating units as requested.

Communication: We communicate through every possible channel with our customers, employees, shareholders, and the financial community.

Citizenship: Worthington Industries practices good citizenship at all levels. We conduct our business in a professional and ethical manner when dealing with customers, neighbors, and the general public worldwide. We encourage all our people to actively participate in community affairs. We support worthwhile community causes.

---

one to travel, however, particularly at the outset. Greater involvement in the work and in the company must become a goal for every employee at every level. All employees must become partners in productivity, improvement, and innovation. Thinking, learning, skill development, and challenge must be designed into every job.

Keep in mind, too, that people can't be *made* to feel that their jobs are valuable or that they are an important part of the business. The only way for that to happen is to give them responsible positions and let them know how their performance impacts the company, its customers, its suppliers, and other stakeholders. The simple truth is that if employees don't play a significant role in the business, you can't fool them into thinking they do.

Of the many ways organizations are trying to improve the performance of their employees, increased accountability is one of the most important. In most cases, if people are accountable for what they do, they'll do it better. Accountability can help provide focus, communicate priorities, indicate serious commitment to an issue, create a sense of urgency and tension, and demonstrate to all those in the organization that its leaders are even-handed and fair. In addition, and perhaps most significantly, recent studies indicate that accountability may be the single most important factor in effective decision making. It's hardly a surprise that people who have to live with the consequences of their decisions tend to make better ones.

The wrong kind of accountability, however, can focus energy on the wrong kind of activities, and can lead to the formation of habits that must be broken. For example, it is common for many managers to be largely accountable for pleasing their bosses or making *their* bosses look good to their bosses. Often, too, managers are held accountable for short-term improvements in performance measurements that are achieved by mortgaging future opportunities; or for meeting agreed-upon performance targets, which may represent an improvement over yesterday's performance, but ignore the possibility of far greater improvement. Meanwhile, at lower levels of the organization, employees are frequently held accountable for complying with standard procedures and doing their job as it was designed to be performed instead of seeking new and more efficient ways of doing the work, innovating the process, and better serving the customer.

Left unchanged, these accountability practices wed us to the past. They make it more rewarding (or at least less punishing) to do things as they have always been done. If, however, we want to provide people with a challenging role in a changing organization, we must design accountability so that it supports that role and encourages that change. The focus needs to be less on immediate (and sometimes mean-ingless) results and more on continuous improvement and learning.

Shifting the Burden of Proof: The Role of Management

Most organizations work from the assumption that management knows best—that managers ought to have control until a convincing argument can be made to the contrary. If lower level employees (or teams) seek greater authority, they must ask for it, then demonstrate that they de-serve it, will use it wisely, and—maybe most importantly—show that transferring the authority will lead to a preferable result. The burden of proof, in other words, lies with the employees.

What if we shifted that burden to management? In this paradigm, the assumption would be that the people (or more likely, teams) who work the process also have complete authority over it and are held ac-countable for its success. Meanwhile, if anyone wants to centralize authority (i.e., move authority further up the hierarchy, assuming there is one), he or she will have to convince the organization that doing so would lead to a preferable outcome. It would also be up to the team to ask for the help it needs, submit its own budgets, measure its own performance, calculate its return on investment to the com-pany, and generally justify that it is worthy of its members' salaries and the organization's decision to entrust it with ownership of the process.

Shifting the burden of proof in this manner represents a major shift in the role of management in most organizations. While incorporating "empowered" teams into a traditional environment is a significant task, shifting the burden of proof is even more of a challenge, demanding entirely different accountability practices and an entirely different envi-ronment. Still, we feel that giving people the type of knee-knocking accountability that puts them at risk—the way that owners are at risk—is an effective alternative to a system that boasts empowerment, but often delivers a great deal less.

The Ability/Accountability Mismatch

Nothing is more unfair than holding someone accountable for something they can't do. Yet, in their rush to extend accountability, this is precisely what many organizations have done (and continue to do). We've asked workers, especially on the front-line, to improve and be accountable for their performance. In many cases, however, we've given them little control over the process, which is frequently the cause of most problems. In other words, the accountability is there, but the individual employee's ability to meet it is not. As a result, workers are often frustrated, customers are disgruntled, and we rarely get the improvement we're looking for.

How can this mismatch between ability and accountability be averted? How can we be certain that accountability is fair and supports our efforts to improve and change? Here are three questions to ask before assigning accountability:

1. *What must be done?* Before people can be held accountable, they must have a clear understanding of what it is they are being held accountable for. People shouldn't be held accountable for performing an activity. Rather, people should be accountable primarily for making a significant contribution.

   Also, more frequently than anyone wants to admit, people are held accountable for tasks not worth performing. Every task for which an individual is to be held accountable must be examined to ensure that it adds value. If a task is not worth doing, don't hold anyone accountable for doing it, *stop* doing it!

2. *Who will be accountable?* Who's responsible? Is it someone or some group? Too often responsibility is unclear. Accountability should be assigned at the lowest level possible. Those closest to customers (or processes) are best equipped to deal with them, and should, therefore, be the ones who are held accountable for the consequences of their actions. When there are teams, there should be team, not individual, accountability. Team members must win or lose as a team.

We're not talking casual accountability here, but genuine "buck-stops-here" accountability. So when the question is asked, "Who's accountable here?" there's a single raised hand, not a half-dozen fingers pointing in every direction. This is not to say that accountability should engender fear, but rather that each person should be responsible for his or her actions. Besides, accountability is inevitably accompanied by a certain amount of discomfort.

3. *What abilities will those being held accountable need to achieve success?* The issues raised by this question are often discussed, but rarely resolved. We've seen few systematic plans to ensure that the right people in the process have sufficient control or the right skills to do the job required. This problem is sometimes compounded by a managerial mindset that often results in managers receiving the lion's share of the benefits of training and education.

The question also arises, "How much ability is enough?" There is no definitive answer. We do know, however, that the ability to succeed today will probably not be adequate a year from now, and that the best companies are focusing their training efforts 12 to 18 months into the future. While some of the skills that these companies invest in today may not be transferable to future processes, learning that will result from broader experiences and education, more experimentation, process improvement skills, and facility in handling information better will enable these companies to adapt to change more quickly, respond with greater flexibility, and shift course more effectively when the time is right.

What *are* the elements that constitute the "ability to succeed?" There is more involved than the formal training we usually associate with making someone "able." Here are some questions to spark discussion about a person's or group's ability to perform specific tasks: To what extent do people or groups have:

Goal Clarity:

- Do they understand customer and other stakeholder interests?
- Do they have a consistent vision of desired outcomes?

- Do they understand the company's strategy and their group's role in the process?

Education and Experience:

- Do they understand the complexities of the task?
- Do they have the ability to anticipate potential problems?
- Do they have the ability to predict the consequences of different courses of action in a variety of circumstances?

Control of the Process:

- Do they have the authority to change or redesign the process as required?
- Do they have the authority to deviate from the process when called for?
- Do they have the authority to influence peers and other departments to achieve needed cooperation?

10

Leaders,
Test Your
Assumptions

> *If you as management are considering the development of a new product or process, you expect without question to devote a lot of time, money, and energy to turning the initial idea into a finished product. However, when we turn to look at the problems of managing people or matters to do with the human side of enterprise, we find management attempting to shortcut the process completely. The assumption is that we can go from idea to product without any intervening development process.*
> —DOUGLAS McGREGOR, *The Professional Manager*

Over the past few decades, there has been a gradual undermining of many organizations and institutions that people have traditionally turned to for a sense of belonging. There's been a notable de-emphasis on the extended family; even the nuclear family has been diminished by separation and divorce. Many people moved away from religion when they saw its leaders not practicing what they preached. Many others became cynical about government when the self-serving actions of elected officials were revealed and when government no longer appeared to work. Long-time political party affiliations were also weakened as parties adopted platforms that were more a response to trends than a reflection of long-held beliefs. More and more of our traditional institutions have become harder to believe in.

Disappointment in our traditional institutions notwithstanding, people all over America are still looking for that worthwhile organization and cause to commit themselves to—and maybe looking harder than ever. One-third of the workforce volunteers more than three hours a week outside the workplace. Many of them work harder for volunteer organizations than they do for the organization that pays them. Many of us die for a cause when precious few would die for money.

These observations go to the very heart of the issue we confront in remaking the workplace into one that is intrinsically motivating. Collectively, we are a people seeking something powerful and meaningful to touch our hearts and minds. We do not respond for long to small, self-centered purposes or to self-aggrandizing work. On the contrary, we are at our best when we are swept up by commitment and are working in the service of a larger goal. We're looking for a cause that fires our imagination and excites our spirit. For the organization that can satisfy these needs—particularly today when there is a dearth of organizations that can—an enormous opportunity exists.

People want a cause that distinguishes them from others. They want leaders that appeal to the nobility in them, rather than the greed in them. They want a compelling reason for having come together—a shared sense of identity and purpose that captures their spirit and fires their imagination. No one gets excited about being average. If we don't stretch our goals, offer a valuable cause, and give people an opportunity to realize their potential, chances are they won't give us the best they have to give. This doesn't mean that every biotech company has to commit to wiping out hunger and starvation on the planet, or that every retailer has to clothe the homeless. Less ambitious causes can make employees proud to be working for the organization. The biotech company can focus on leading the industry in developing environmentally friendly products that replace traditional pesticides, while the retailer can content itself with striving to offer the best service in town. The measure of a worthwhile cause is not how lofty it sounds to an outsider or how it assuages the social conscience or stimulates the competitive juices of the management council. A good cause is one that excites employees, deepens their commitment, and lends meaning to their work.

While such a cause is rare in many organizations, we don't have to look far to see cause-driven individuals in action—just check out the evening news. Most likely, somewhere in the country emergency crews are fighting howling winds, flooding waters, or raging fires. There's danger everywhere, the crew members have been on the job for 30 hours straight, yet morale is up, performance levels are up, and complaints are negligible. Meanwhile, on another front, the Coast Guard is on a search-and-rescue mission, braving churning seas, near-zero visibility, and a low probability of success in the hunt for a missing fishing boat. Yet, they persist in the face of incredible odds. Their cause is clear, their commitment total.

Give these same individuals a job in most companies and you'd think that you were witnessing totally different people—and not just because they work at a desk or have a sales route. Rather, it is because they feel that the work they are doing is simply not worthy of their best efforts.

Build Core Values That Guide Performance

> *It is really fantastic to me that one book after another will make a pious statement about this new development and about organizational theory and management theory and then proceed to say nothing whatsoever about values and purpose except in some vague way that any high school senior could match.*
> —ABRAHAM MASLOW, *Maslow on Management*, 1999

A company's values are its code of ethics, its behavioral framework. Taken together, they form a statement of what the organization collectively deems important or valuable—what it stands for. When understood and adopted by employees, values provide a context for action. Values can provide a sense of order without rules, reduce ambiguity without a detailed plan, and bring focus and coherence while allowing individual expression and self-determination.

Most organizations have a published set of values. They are usually well-written and widely communicated—and are a significant source of frustration. Why? Because it is a rare company today in which people practice the values their organization preaches. Just listen to the grumbling at coffee breaks, read between the lines at the next employee meeting, or read the verbatims on the employee survey—the gap between our professed values and our values in practice is significant.

If respecting the individual is a core value, why do we promote so many people who are technical experts but have lousy people skills? And why do we tolerate managers who get results but are frequently disrespectful to people in their work groups?

- If we value cooperation and teamwork, why have we designed so many structures that reward people for competing more than cooperating?
- If every employee is encouraged to seek excellence, why do we still have so many uninteresting, narrowly defined jobs? Why is training the first thing to be cut when money is tight?
- If providing the best possible service to customers is a core value, why do we make so many rules that make it hard for employees to meet customers' needs?
- If we have adopted a total quality approach, why are so few senior managers actively involved in the effort?

And the list goes on. Our failure to measure the extent to which we live up to our espoused values has made it easy for many to overlook how often we do not "walk the talk." The result has been lower levels of trust, greater confusion and frustration, and less sense of community among employees in many organizations. People genuinely want their company to stand for something. And, when it does, it increases people's feelings that their organization is special. The first step in closing the gap as it relates to values is to choose to get serious about doing so. Look at the values you've published. Just how committed are you to acting within this framework? If a person purposely acts in a manner inconsistent with these values, what is the likely consequence? Dismissal? Coach and counsel? It's an easy decision when an employee steals from the company. But what if one of your core values is respect and a long-time supervisor is clearly and consistently disrespectful of an employee in front of the work group? When this supervisor keeps his or her job after acting disrespectfully, what is the message sent to others in the organization about the importance of core values?

It's difficult to be truly tough on values. But perhaps we have let the pendulum swing too far in the "give-'em-another-chance" direction. If there isn't significant accountability for the clear and deliberate abuse of values, then there are no values. On the other hand, when you do take action, when people who don't live the values are asked to leave, there is usually little, if any, mourning.

If we're not going to live our values, we would be better off not listing them. The only thing worse than not having a set of guidelines to provide order to behavior within the system is to have a visible set of values that are situationally enforced or largely ignored. In these cases, employees are reminded daily of how little leaders in the company can be trusted to keep their word. Values must be every organization's North Star—an ever-visible guide that employees can look to, in order to tell whether they are acting in ways that promote the organizational good.

To be effective, values must be:

- Profound enough to touch the hearts and minds of all employees, yet simple enough to be readily understood.
- Concrete enough to provide a useful framework for decision making.
- Pragmatic enough and sufficiently consistent with organizational structures to be reinforced in normal day-to-day activities.

- Communicated over time in every aspect of the business.
- Reinforced through accountability.

Commit to the Truth and Share a Sense of Reality

> *If man is not what conventional organizational*
> *theory assumes him to be, then much of the*
> *organization planning carried on within the*
> *framework of that theory is nothing more than*
> *a game of logic. The organization chart, the*
> *position, the descriptions, and the control*
> *policies all become elaborate and formal ways of*
> *stating what people would do if human nature*
> *were what it is believed to be. What we find*
> *when we study human behavior in*
> *organizations is that people do not behave in*
> *the way the logical theory says they should*
> *behave. In fact, we discover the existence of an*
> *informal organization which shows us that*
> *people are violating the conventional principles*
> *of organization constantly, and in a great*
> *many ways.*
> —DOUGLAS McGREGOR, *The Professional Manager*

No matter how empathetic we are (or think we are) as leaders, no matter how open, the organizational deck is stacked against us. When we are liked, people often color the information they give us because they don't want to disappoint us and they don't want to complain. If they fear our reaction (either because of our past actions or our position), very little information about the less than positive aspects of the current situation is volunteered. Most of us have felt the pressure to not be "too negative" or to ensure that bad news is balanced with enough positive information even if this requires coloring or recasting reality. The expression "You tell the boss" didn't evolve because people were reluctant to be rewarded but because they didn't want to experience the boss's reaction.

In most organizations, people are biased toward the way they *wish* things were, not as things are. The choice to avoid the truth is not always a conscious one and is often quite subtle. Just look at the number of ways people in your organization are implicitly (and sometimes even explicitly) rewarded for making things sound better than they are or telling their bosses what they think their bosses want to hear. Bad news doesn't travel up quickly in most organizations, but it should. By selectively modifying reality, we falsely diminish people's understanding of "the gap" and, therefore, rob the organization of the sense of urgency and creative tension that will be required to focus and sustain improvement efforts.

Developing a shared sense of reality must be a strategic issue. It is exceedingly difficult to change reality if you don't see it or if there is no agreement on what "real" is. We must recognize the effect present structures have on our willingness and ability to see reality, and we must search out and eliminate those practices that make it safer or more rewarding to do anything but "tell it like it is."

As part of seeing that reality with greater clarity, we must continue to contemplate new information and strive to see old information in new ways. Thinking, it is said, is a matter of rearranging our prejudices, and without new information to challenge our thought processes, our tendency will be to merely reinforce the prejudices we have. We must also encourage everyone in the organization to ask the difficult questions—those that challenge the system and "business as usual"—and work to create an environment where questions are welcomed. Just as we encourage children and students to ask questions because we want them to be avid learners, we must encourage and support avid learning in the workplace.

And just in case we want a reality check on our change efforts to determine whether what we think or hope is happening truly is,

we don't have to develop a customer survey or hire an outside consultant. For a fair and candid review of what's really happening in our
organization, we need only to check with the employees on the front
line. If our own consulting work with literally hundreds of corporations has taught us anything, it is that the front line never lies.

Part 2

Selected Essays of Douglas McGregor

McGregor's Human Side of Enterprise

Out of all this has come the first clear
recognition of an inescapable fact: we cannot
successfully force people to work for
management's objectives. The ancient
conception that people do the work of the
world only if they are forced to do so by
threats or intimidation, or by the camouflaged
authoritarian methods of paternalism, has
been suffering from a lingering fatal illness for
a quarter of a century. I venture to guess that
it will be dead in another decade.

—DOUGLAS McGREGOR, *The Professional Manager*

Douglas McGregor coined the terms Theory X and Theory Y to describe a set of assumptions or propositions managers developed about people and their capabilities and potential. He drew heavily from the work of famed psychologist Abraham Maslow and based much of the famous X and Y on Maslow's theory of motivation.

Douglas McGregor went on to write his best selling book, *The Human Side of Enterprise*. From that day forward, the great debates began between Douglas McGregor and Abraham Maslow. Both men died imploring every leader to look into the mirror and question their assumptions. Their questions, although a decade old, seem perfect for today's new world of work:

1. Do you believe that people are trustworthy?
2. Do you believe that people seek responsibility and accountability?
3. Do you believe that people naturally want to learn?
4. Do you believe that people seek meaning in their work?
5. Do you believe that people don't resist change but they resist being changed?
6. Do you believe that people prefer work to being idle?

Our answers to these questions form the foundation of our assumptions about people. McGregor's original essay on building the human side of enterprise is filled with much of the wisdom we are searching for today in our quest to build organizations that are capable of rapid change, technological innovation, and innovation.

The Human Side of Enterprise

It has become trite to say that the most significant developments of the next quarter century will take place not in the physical but in the social sciences, that industry—the economic organ of society—has the fundamental know-how to utilize physical science and technology for the material benefit of mankind, and that we must now learn how to utilize the social sciences to make our human organizations truly effective.

Many people agree in principle with such statements; but so far they represent a pious hope—and little else. Consider with me, if you will, something of what may be involved when we attempt to transform the hope into reality.

I

Let me begin with an analogy. A quarter century ago basic conceptions of the nature of matter and energy had changed profoundly from what they had been since Newton's time. The physical scientists were persuaded that under proper conditions new and hitherto unimagined sources of energy could be made available to mankind.

We know what has happened since then. First came the bomb. Then, during the past decade, have come many other attempts to exploit these scientific discoveries—some successful, some not.

First published in *Adventure in Thought and Action,* Proceedings of the Fifth Anniversary Convocation of the School of Industrial Management, Massachusetts Institute of Technology, Cambridge, April 9, 1957. Cambridge, Mass.: M.I.T. School of Industrial Management, 1957; and reprinted in *The Management Review,* 1957, 46, No. 11, 22–28.

The point of my analogy, however, is that the application of theory in this field is a slow and costly matter. We expect it always to be thus. No one is impatient with the scientist because he cannot tell industry how to build a simple, cheap, all-purpose source of atomic energy today. That it will take at least another decade and the investment of billions of dollars to achieve results which are economically competitive with present sources of power is understood and accepted.

It is transparently pretentious to suggest any *direct* similarity between the developments in the physical sciences leading to the harnessing of atomic energy and potential developments in the social sciences. Nevertheless, the analogy is not as absurd as it might appear to be at first glance.

To a lesser degree, and in a much more tentative fashion, we are in a position in the social sciences today like that of the physical sciences with respect to atomic energy in the thirties. We know that past conceptions of the nature of man are inadequate and in many ways incorrect. We are becoming quite certain that, under proper conditions, unimagined resources of creative human energy could become available within the organizational setting.

We cannot tell industrial management how to apply this new knowledge in simple, economic ways. We know it will require years of exploration, much costly development research, and a substantial amount of creative imagination on the part of management to discover how to apply this growing knowledge to the organization of human effort in industry.

May I ask that you keep this analogy in mind—overdrawn and pretentious though it may be—as a framework for what I have to say this morning.

Management's Task: Conventional View

The conventional conception of management's task in harnessing human energy to organizational requirements can be stated broadly in terms of three propositions. In order to avoid the complications introduced by a label, I shall call this set of propositions "Theory X":

1. Management is responsible for organizing the elements of productive enterprise—money, materials, equipment, people—in the interest of economic ends.
2. With respect to people, this is a process of directing their efforts, motivating them, controlling their actions, modifying their behavior to fit the needs of the organization.
3. Without this active intervention by management, people would be passive—even resistant—to organizational needs. They must therefore be persuaded, rewarded, punished, controlled—their activities must be directed. This is management's task—in managing subordinate managers or workers. We often sum it up by saying that management consists of getting things done through other people.

Behind this conventional theory there are several additional beliefs— less explicit, but widespread:

4. The average man is by nature indolent—he works as little as possible.
5. He lacks ambition, dislikes responsibility, prefers to be led.
6. He is inherently self-centered, indifferent to organizational needs.
7. He is by nature resistant to change.
8. He is gullible, not very bright, the ready dupe of the charlatan and the demagogue.

The human side of economic enterprise today is fashioned from propositions and beliefs such as these. Conventional organization structures, managerial policies, practices, and programs reflect these assumptions.

In accomplishing its task—with these assumptions as guides—management has conceived of a range of possibilities between two extremes.

The Hard or the Soft Approach?

At one extreme, management can be "hard" or "strong." The methods for directing behavior involve coercion and threat (usually disguised), close supervision, tight controls over behavior. At the other extreme, management can be "soft" or "weak." The methods for directing behavior involve being permissive, satisfying people's demands, achieving harmony. Then they will be tractable, accept direction.

This range has been fairly completely explored during the past half century, and management has learned some things from the exploration. There are difficulties in the "hard" approach. Force breeds counterforces: restriction of output, antagonism, militant unionism, subtle but effective sabotage of management objectives. This approach is especially difficult during times of full employment.

There are also difficulties in the "soft" approach. It leads frequently to the abdication of management—to harmony, perhaps, but to indifferent performance. People take advantage of the soft approach. They continually expect more, but they give less and less.

Currently, the popular theme is "firm but fair." This is an attempt to gain the advantages of both the hard and the soft approaches. It is reminiscent of Teddy Roosevelt's "speak softly and carry a big stick."

Is the Conventional View Correct?

The findings which are beginning to emerge from the social sciences challenge this whole set of beliefs about man and human nature and about the task of management. The evidence is far from conclusive, certainly, but it is suggestive. It comes from the laboratory, the clinic, the schoolroom, the home, and even to a limited extent from industry itself.

The social scientist does not deny that human behavior in industrial organization today is approximately what management perceives it to be. He has, in fact, observed it and studied it fairly extensively. But he is pretty sure that this behavior is *not* a consequence of man's inherent nature. It is a consequence rather of the nature of industrial organizations, of management philosophy, policy, and practice. The conventional approach of Theory X is based on mistaken notions of what is cause and what is effect.

"Well," you ask, "what then is the *true* nature of man? What evidence leads the social scientist to deny what is obvious?" And, if I am not mistaken, you are also thinking, "Tell me—simply, and without a lot of scientific verbiage—what you think you know that is so unusual. Give me—without a lot of intellectual claptrap and theoretical nonsense—some practical ideas which will enable me to improve the situation in my organization. And remember, I'm faced with increasing costs and narrowing profit margins. I want proof that such ideas won't result simply in new and costly human relations frills. I want practical results, and I want them now."

If these are your wishes, you are going to be disappointed. Such requests can no more be met by the social scientist today than could comparable ones with respect to atomic energy be met by the physicist fifteen years ago. I can, however, indicate a few of the reasons for asserting that conventional assumptions about the human side of enterprise are inadequate. And I can suggest—tentatively—some of the propositions that will compose a more adequate theory of the management of people. The magnitude of the task that confronts us will then, I think, be apparent.

II

Perhaps the best way to indicate why the conventional approach of management is inadequate is to consider the subject of motivation. In discussing this subject I will draw heavily on the work of my colleague, Abraham Maslow of Brandeis University. His is the most fruitful approach I know. Naturally, what I have to say will be overgeneralized and will ignore important qualifications. In the time at our disposal, this is inevitable.

Physiological and Safety Needs

Man is a wanting animal—as soon as one of his needs is satisfied, another appears in its place. This process is unending. It continues from birth to death.

Man's needs are organized in a series of levels—a hierarchy of importance. At the lowest level, but preeminent in importance when they are thwarted, are his physiological needs. Man lives by bread alone, when there is not bread. Unless the circumstances are unusual, his needs for love, for status, for recognition are inoperative when his stomach has been empty for a while. But when he eats regularly and adequately, hunger ceases to be an important need. The sated man has hunger only in the sense that a full bottle has emptiness. The same is true of the other physiological needs of man—for rest, exercise, shelter, protection from the elements.

A satisfied need is not a motivator of behavior! This is a fact of profound significance. It is a fact that is regularly ignored in the conventional approach to the management of people. I shall return to it later. For the moment, one example will make my point. Consider your own need for air. Except as you are deprived of it, it has no appreciable motivating effect upon your behavior.

When the physiological needs are reasonably satisfied, needs at the next higher level begin to dominate man's behavior—to motivate him. These are called safety needs. They are needs for protection against danger, threat, deprivation. Some people mistakenly refer to these as needs for security. However, unless man is in a dependent relationship where he fears arbitrary deprivation, he does not demand security. The need is for the "fairest possible break." When he is confident of this, he is more than willing to take risks. But when he feels threatened or dependent, his greatest need is for guarantees, for protection, for security.

The fact needs little emphasis that, since every industrial employee is in a dependent relationship, safety needs may assume considerable importance. Arbitrary management actions, behavior that arouses uncertainty with respect to continued employment or which reflects favoritism or discrimination, unpredictable administration of policy—these will be powerful motivators of the safety needs in the employment relationship at every level from worker to vice president.

Social Needs

When man's physiological needs are satisfied and he is no longer fearful about his physical welfare, his social needs become important motivators of his behavior—for belonging, for association, for acceptance by his fellows, for giving and receiving friendship and love.

Management knows today of the existence of these needs, but it often assumes quite wrongly that they represent a threat to the organization. Many studies have demonstrated that the tightly knit, cohesive work group may, under proper conditions, be far more effective than an equal number of separate individuals in achieving organizational goals.

Yet management, fearing group hostility to its own objectives, often goes to considerable lengths to control and direct human efforts in ways that are inimical to the natural "groupiness" of human beings. When man's social needs—and perhaps his safety needs, too—are thus thwarted, he behaves in ways which tend to defeat organizational objectives. He becomes resistant, antagonistic, uncooperative. But this behavior is a consequence, not a cause.

Ego Needs

Above the social needs—in the sense that they do not become motivators until lower needs are reasonably satisfied—are the needs of greatest significance to management and to man himself. They are the egoistic needs, and they are of two kinds:

1. Those needs that relate to one's self esteem needs for self-confidence, for independence, for achievement, for competence, for knowledge.
2. Those needs that relate to one's reputation—needs for status, for recognition, for appreciation, for the deserved respect of one's fellows.

Unlike the lower needs, these are rarely satisfied; man seeks indefinitely for more satisfaction of these needs once they have become important to him. But they do not appear in any significant way until physiological, safety, and social needs are all reasonably satisfied.

The typical industrial organization offers few opportunities for the satisfaction of these egoistic needs to people at lower levels in the hierarchy. The conventional methods of organizing work, particularly in mass-production industries, give little heed to these aspects of human motivation. If the practices of scientific management were deliberately calculated to thwart these needs—which, of course, they are not—they could hardly accomplish this purpose better than they do.

Self-Fulfillment Needs

Finally—a capstone, as it were, on the hierarchy of man's needs—there are what we may call the needs for self-fulfillment. These are the needs for realizing one's own potentialities, for continued self-development, for being creative in the broadest sense of that term.

It is clear that the conditions of modern life give only limited opportunity for these relatively weak needs to obtain expression. The deprivation most people experience with respect to other lower-level needs diverts their energies into the struggle to satisfy *those* needs, and the needs for self-fulfillment remain dormant.

III

Now, briefly, a few general comments about motivation:

We recognize readily enough that a man suffering from a severe dietary deficiency is sick. The deprivation of physiological needs has behavioral consequences. The same is true—although less well organized—of deprivation of higher-level needs. The man whose needs for safety, association, independence, or status are thwarted is sick just as surely as is he who has rickets. And his sickness will have behavioral consequences. We will be mistaken if we attribute his resultant passivity, his hostility, his refusal to accept responsibility to his inherent "human nature." These forms of behavior are *symptoms* of illness—of deprivation of his social and egoistic needs.

The man whose lower-level needs are satisfied is not motivated to satisfy those needs any longer. For practical purposes they exist no longer. (Remember my point about your need for air.) Management often asks, "Why aren't people more productive? We pay good wages, provide good working conditions, have excellent fringe benefits and steady employment. Yet people do not seem to be willing to put forth more than minimum effort."

The fact that management has provided for these physiological and safety needs has shifted the motivational emphasis to the social and perhaps to the egoistic needs. Unless there are opportunities *at work* to satisfy these higher-level needs, people will be deprived; and their behavior will reflect this deprivation. Under such conditions, if management continues to focus its attention on physiological needs, its efforts are bound to be ineffective.

People *will* make insistent demands for more money under these conditions. It becomes more important than ever to buy the material goods and services that can provide limited satisfaction of the thwarted needs. Although money has only limited value in satisfying many higher-level needs, it can become the focus of interest if it is the *only* means available.

The Carrot-and-Stick Approach

The carrot-and-stick theory of motivation (like Newtonian physical theory) works reasonably well under certain circumstances. The *means* for satisfying man's physiological and (within limits) his safety needs can be provided or withheld by management. Employment itself is such a means, and so are wages, working conditions, and benefits. By these means the individual can be controlled so long as he is struggling for subsistence. Man lives for bread alone when there is no bread.

But the carrot-and-stick theory does not work at all once man has reached an adequate subsistence level and is motivated primarily by higher needs. Management cannot provide a man with self-respect, or with the respect of his fellows, or with the satisfaction of needs for self-fulfillment. It can create conditions such that he is encouraged and enabled to seek such satisfactions *for himself,* or it can thwart him by failing to create those conditions.

But this creation of conditions is not "control." It is not a good device for directing behavior. And so management finds itself in an odd position. The high standard of living created by our modern technological know-how provides quite adequately for the satisfaction of physiological and safety needs. The only significant exception is where management practices have not created confidence in a "fair break"—and thus where safety needs are thwarted. But by making possible the satisfaction of low-level needs, management has deprived itself of the ability to use as motivators the devices on which conventional theory has taught it to rely—rewards, promises, incentives, or threats and other coercive devices.

Neither Hard nor Soft

The philosophy of management by direction and control—*regardless of whether it is hard or soft*—is inadequate to motivate, because the human needs on which this approach relies are today unimportant motivators of behavior. Direction and control are essentially useless in motivating people whose important needs are social and egoistic. Both the hard and the soft approach fail today because they are simply irrelevant to the situation.

People deprived of opportunities to satisfy at work the needs that are now important to them behave exactly as we might predict—with indolence, passivity, resistance to change, lack of responsibility, willingness to follow the demagogue, unreasonable demands for economic benefits. It would seem that we are caught in a web of our own weaving.

In summary, then, of these comments about motivation:

Management by direction and control—whether implemented with the hard, the soft, or the firm but fair approach—fails under today's conditions to provide effective motivation of human effort toward organizational objectives. It fails because direction and control are useless methods of motivating people whose physiological and safety needs are reasonably satisfied and whose social, egoistic, and self-fulfillment needs are predominant.

IV

For these and many other reasons, we require a different theory of the task of managing people based on more adequate assumptions about human nature and human motivation. I am going to be so bold as to suggest the broad dimensions of such a theory. Call it "Theory Y," if you will.

1. Management is responsible for organizing the elements of productive enterprise—money, materials, equipment, people—in the interest of economic ends.
2. People are *not* by nature passive or resistant to organizational needs. They have become so as a result of experience in organizations.
3. The motivation, the potential for development, the capacity for assuming responsibility, the readiness to direct behavior toward organizational goals are all present in people. Management does not put them there. It is a responsibility of management to make it possible for people to recognize and develop these human characteristics for themselves.
4. The essential task of management is to arrange organizational conditions and methods of operation so that people can achieve their own goals *best* by directing *their own* efforts toward organizational objectives.

This is a process primarily of creating opportunities, releasing potential, removing obstacles, encouraging growth, providing guidance. It is what Peter Drucker has called "management by objectives" in contract to "management by control."

And I hasten to add that it does *not* involve the abdication of management, the absence of leadership, the lowering of standards, or the other characteristics usually associated with the "soft" approach under

Theory X. Much to the contrary. It is no more possible to create an organization today which will be a fully effective application of this theory than it was to build an atomic power plant in 1945. There are many formidable obstacles to overcome.

Some Difficulties

The conditions imposed by conventional organization theory and by the approach of scientific management for the past half century have tied men to limited jobs which did not utilize their capabilities, have discouraged the acceptance of responsibility, have encouraged passivity, have eliminated meaning from work. Man's habits, attitudes, expectations— his whole conception of membership in an industrial organization—have been conditioned by his experience under these circumstances. Change in the direction of Theory Y will be slow, and it will require extensive modification of the attitudes of management and workers alike.

People today are accustomed to being directed, manipulated, controlled in industrial organizations and to finding satisfaction for their social, egoistic, and self-fulfillment needs away from the job. This is true of much of management as well as of workers. Genuine "industrial citizenship"—to borrow again a term from Drucker—is a remote and unrealistic idea, the meaning of which has not even been considered by most members of industrial organizations.

Another way of saying this is that Theory X places exclusive reliance upon external control of human behavior, whereas Theory Y relies heavily on self-control and self-direction. It is worth noting that this difference is the difference between treating people as children and treating them as mature adults. After generations of the former, we cannot expect to shift to the latter overnight.

V

Before we are overwhelmed by the obstacles, let us remember that the application of theory is always slow. Progress is usually achieved in small steps.

Consider with me a few innovative ideas which are entirely consistent with Theory Y and which are today being applied with some success.

Decentralization and Delegation

These are ways of freeing people from the too-close control of conventional organization, giving them a degree of freedom to direct their own activities, to assume responsibility, and, importantly, to satisfy their egoistic needs. In this connection, the flat organization of Sears, Roebuck and Company provides an interesting example. It forces "management by objectives" since it enlarges the number of people reporting to a manager until he cannot direct and control them in the conventional manner.

Job Enlargement

This concept, pioneered by I.B.M. and Detroit Edison, is quite consistent with Theory Y. It encourages the acceptance of responsibility at the bottom of the organization; it provides opportunities for satisfying social and egoistic needs. In fact, the reorganization of work at the factory level offers one of the more challenging opportunities for innovation consistent with Theory Y. The studies by A. T. M. Wilson and his associates of British coal mining and Indian textile manufacture have added appreciably to our understanding of work organization. Moreover, the economic and psychological results achieved by this work have been substantial.

Participation and Consultative Management

Under proper conditions these results provide encouragement to people to direct their creative energies toward organizational objectives, give them some voice in decisions that affect them, provide significant opportunities for the satisfaction of social and egoistic needs. I need only mention the Scanlon Plan as the outstanding embodiment of these ideas in practice.

The not infrequent failure of such ideas as these to work as well as expected is often attributable to the fact that a management has "bought the idea" but applied it within the framework of Theory X and its assumptions.

Delegation is not an effective way of exercising management by control. Participation becomes a farce when it is applied as a sales gimmick or a device for kidding people into thinking they are important. Only the management that has confidence in human capacities and is itself directed toward organizational objectives rather than toward the preservation of personal power can grasp the implications of this emerging theory. Such management will find and apply successfully other innovative ideas as we move slowly toward the full implementation of a theory like Y.

Performance Appraisal

Before I stop, let me mention one other practical application of Theory Y which—though still highly tentative—may well have important consequences. This has to do with performance appraisal within the ranks of management. Even a cursory examination of conventional programs of performance appraisal will reveal how completely consistent they are with Theory X. In fact, most such programs tend to treat the individual as though he were a product under inspection on the assembly line.

Take the typical plan: substitute "product" for "subordinate being appraised," substitute "inspector" for "superior making the appraisal," substitute "rework" for "training or development," and, except for the attributes being judged, the human appraisal process will be virtually indistinguishable from the product-inspection process.

A few companies—among them General Mills, Ansul Chemical, and General Electric—have been experimenting with approaches which involve the individual in setting "targets" or objectives *for himself* and in a *self*-evaluation of performance semiannually or annually. Of course, the superior plays an important leadership role in this process—one, in fact, that demands substantially more competence than the conventional approach. The role is, however, considerably more congenial to many managers than the role of "judge" or "inspector" which is forced upon them by conventional performance. Above all, the individual is encouraged to take a greater responsibility for planning and appraising his own contribution to organizational objectives; and the accompanying effects on egoistic and self-fulfillment needs are substantial. This approach to performance appraisal represents one more innovative idea being explored by a few managements who are moving toward the implementation of Theory Y.

VI

And now I am back where I began. I share the belief that we could realize substantial improvements in the effectiveness of industrial organizations during the next decade or two. Moreover, I believe the social sciences can contribute much to such developments. We are only beginning to grasp the implications of the growing body of knowledge in these fields. But if this conviction is to become a reality instead of a pious hope, we will need to view the process much as we view the process of releasing the energy of the atom for constructive human ends— as a slow, costly, sometimes discouraging approach toward a goal which would seem to many to be quite unrealistic.

The ingenuity and the perseverance of industrial management in the pursuit of economic ends have changed many scientific and technological dreams into commonplace realities. It is now becoming clear that the application of these same talents to the human side of enterprise will not only enhance substantially these materialistic achievements but will bring us one step closer to "the good society." Shall we get on with the job?

New Concepts of Management

*Intellectual creativity cannot be
"programmed" and directed the way we
program and direct an assembly line or an
accounting department. This kind of
intellectual contribution to the enterprise
cannot be obtained by giving orders, by
traditional supervisory practices, or by close
systems of control. Even conventional notions
of productivity are meaningless with reference
to the creative intellectual effort. Management
has not yet considered in any depth what is
involved in managing an organization heavily
populated with people whose prime
contribution consists of creative intellectual
effort. . . .*

—DOUGLAS McGREGOR, *The Professional Manager*

Douglas McGregor predicted in the late 1950s that managers
would witness some profound and far-reaching changes in the
management of people within organizations. McGregor's pro-
phetic essay, "New Concepts of Management," speaks clearly to
our needs today in the workplace. Human resources, the management and development of human capital, and our need to
spark creativity and innovation within organizations are topics
for discussion in companies large and small.

In the following essay, McGregor discusses the needs of
creative professionals that mirror the people practices of many
forward-thinking companies. McGregor also predicted that creativity and innovation would necessitate a need to change the

Read at a conference on "Executive Responsibilities in a Period of Exploding Technology," which was held at M.I.T.; and published in *The Technology Review*, 1961,
63, No. 4, 2–4.

deep-seated and long-standing concept of managerial control. In its place, McGregor believed that self-direction and self-control was the only opportunity for management to realize the full potential of employees. It was for this reason that McGregor predicted there would be an almost revolutionary change in managerial strategy.

Today we need look no further than Silicon Valley as a laboratory for McGregor's thinking on the new concepts of management. Firms such as Hewlett Packard, Cisco Systems, Peoplesoft, Sun Microsystems, and Yahoo! have implemented many of the concepts McGregor spoke of nearly three decades ago. In an effort to unleash creativity and spur innovation, the revolution McGregor speaks of in this essay may have begun to take place.

I share with a number of colleagues in the field of management, and with a few managers, the conviction that we will witness during the next couple of decades some profound, far-reaching changes in the strategy utilized to manage the human resources of enterprise. These changes will not be superficial modifications in current practice, but basic revisions of certain concepts that have dominated management thinking during the past half century or more.

The circumstances that will ultimately force these changes are already developing, but their significance is not yet widely recognized. They can be summed up in terms of four trends that are clearly apparent in our society today:

1. *The explosive growth of science* (both behavioral and physical), which is yielding knowledge relevant to every function of enterprise—finance, sales, advertising, public relations, personnel, purchasing, manufacturing—as well as research and engineering.
2. *The rapidly increasing complexity of technology* in both office and factory—and in related aspects of everyday life such as transportation and communication.

3. *The growing complexity of industry-society relationships* with government, consumers, suppliers, unions, stockholders, and the public generally. As a result of world-wide economic development, relations with other cultures will add substantially to these complexities.

4. *The changing composition of the industrial work force.* Today more than half the employees of industry in the United States are white-collar. Within the white-collar group, we are witnessing a rapid growth of "exempt" salaried personnel, which includes managers and professionally trained people of all kinds. In one large company, the exempt salaried group has grown from 19 per cent to 35 per cent of total employment in the last decade. The curve is accelerating in line with Parkinson's law, but for reasons other than his witty analysis would suggest.

One major consequence of these trends is that in a few years the single largest and most influential class of employees in most industrial organizations will be professional managers and specialists of many kinds, populating every department and every function. Their utilization of various branches of scientific knowledge to solve practical problems will be the primary basis for planning, decision making, and policy formulation from top to bottom of the organization. As a result of the first three trends I have mentioned, they will be both indispensable and powerful, and the necessity to make full use of their competence and training will force a revolution in managerial strategy.

The conventional strategy of management—and the policies and practices as well as organization structures that have developed to serve it—was evolved with the blue-collar wage earner as its primary object. Even he is changing substantially in his education, economic status, attitudes, and competence. But the primary problems of the next several decades will center around the professional specialist. Our present strategy, policies, and practices are quite inappropriate to the task of directing and controlling his efforts. Briefly, let us see why.

Intellectual Creativity

The first and most important reason is the nature of the professional's contribution to the success of the enterprise. His work consists essentially of creative intellectual effort to aid management in its policy making, problem solving, planning, decision making, and administrative activities.

Such professional work cannot be "programmed" and directed the way we program and direct an assembly line or an accounting department. The methods of the industrial engineer are simply irrelevant to it. The management of such work consists chiefly in establishing objectives—the hoped-for results—and in obtaining the professional's commitment to them. It is part of the professional's unique value that he is capable of determining the steps necessary to achieve the desired objectives. Often he knows more about this than his boss does.

This kind of intellectual contribution to the enterprise cannot be obtained by giving orders, by traditional supervisory practices, or by close systems of control, such as we now apply to blue-collar and clerical workers. Even conventional notions of productivity—based as they are on concepts of effort per small unit of time such as the hour or day—are meaningless with reference to the creative intellectual effort of the professional specialist.

In addition, the complexity of the problems to be solved, the nature of the decisions to be made, frequently will demand collaborative effort by many professional specialists from *different* fields ranging clear across the behavioral, biological, and physical sciences. As yet, management has acquired but little knowledge or skill with respect to the management of such collaborative teams, or in developing organizational structures that will provide for their effective utilization.

There has been considerable interest in recent years in "creativity," but this interest has centered on identifying people with creative potential and on such gimmicks as brainstorming. Management has not yet considered in any depth what is involved in *managing* an organization heavily populated with people whose prime contribution consists of creative intellectual effort.

Professional specialists are human beings, of course, but their values, their expectations, and their needs are substantially different from those of the blue-collar worker on whom we have lavished our attention in the past.

What Professionals Want

Economic rewards are certainly important to the professional, but there is ample research to demonstrate that they do not provide the *primary* incentive to peak performance. Management's real task with respect to economic rewards is to administer them in ways that professional employees accept as *equitable*, in order to avoid dissatisfactions and preoccupations that interfere with performance. If they are poorly administered, economic rewards can *lower* productivity below a modest, satisfactory level; they do not appear to be particularly potent in raising it above that level.

Much more crucial to the professional—*provided economic rewards are equitable*—are such things as:

Full utilization of his talent and training, which means critical attention to the nature of his work, the organization of the functions in which he participates, the challenge built into his job, and his freedom from close and detailed supervision.

His status, not only within the organization but externally with respect to his profession. Our tendency to regard staff functions, where most professionals reside, as "burdens" on production is but one way in which we prevent him from achieving status.

In addition, despite some rather paternalistic concessions such as permission to attend professional society meetings, management tends to bind the professional to the enterprise in a fashion that minimizes his opportunity to achieve status and recognition among his colleagues in his field. Publication, and participation in the affairs of professional societies are far more important sources of status than mere attendance at meetings. Yet, even where competitive secrets are not involved, such activities often are regarded as undesirable distractions from the professional's primary responsibilities to his company. In fact, they contribute to his value, as well as to his status and satisfaction.

His opportunities for development within his professional career.
Our elaborate programs for *management* development provide few opportunities today for the *career* development of professional specialists.

Conventional policies and practices with respect to promotion penalize the man who does not aspire to a managerial job, by requiring him to change his function and assume different responsibilities. Promotion, for the professional, means receiving rewards and recognition for doing better exactly what he has been doing already. Management has given little heed to these values of the professional so far, or to their policy implications. The professional's long-term career expectations are of fundamental importance to him. In private practice or in academic institutions, he is accustomed to choosing among alternative opportunities in terms of these values. Industrial management, on the other hand, is accustomed to exercising a substantial amount of "career authority" over its managerial employees at all levels. The individual is evaluated, promoted, rotated, and transferred in terms of the needs of the organization almost irrespective of his personal career motivations. These incompatible points of view are certain to come into conflict as professional employees become more numerous and more indispensable to industry.

This inconsistency, it is worth noting, has political implications of more than minor significance. One of the distinguishing features of our Western democratic society, we proudly affirm, is that the individual is *not* the servant of the state. It is interesting that the largest and most powerful institution in this same Western society—industry—characteristically administers promotion policies (which profoundly affect the lifetime careers of its employees) with almost complete emphasis on "the needs of the organization." Only his freedom to quit—a freedom that is often too costly to exercise after he has built up a substantial equity in company benefit plans—protects the individual from being in fact "a servant of the corporation" in this rather basic way.

Two Qualifications

Among the qualifications that should be discussed, with respect to these generalizations, two must be mentioned to prevent misunderstanding.

First, I have talked about a class of people—professional specialists—as though they were all alike, all possessed of the same attitudes, expectations, values, and needs. Obviously, they are not; like any other class of human beings, they differ one from the other in every one of the respects I have mentioned.

Behavioral scientists have studied two groups of professionals lying at the extremes of a range. At one extreme are the "locals" who readily adjust their values and aspirations to the organization that employs them. At the other end are the "cosmopolitans" whose primary identification is with their professional field regardless of where they are employed. Note, however, that there is no evidence to indicate that competence, ability, or potential contribution to the organization are localized in any one part of this range. The comments I have made about professionals should be taken as applying broadly to the middle of the continuum.

Second, although I have directed your attention to a single class of employees, it is obvious that the trends in our society will affect other groups as well. Line managers, for example, will themselves inevitably become more professional, both in training and outlook. The work of wage earners and clerical personnel, as well as their attitudes and expectations, will be materially affected. The growth in numbers and influence of professional specialists in every function of the business will nevertheless be the most dramatic of these changes, and the one requiring the most drastic alterations in management strategy.

Self-Direction Is Essential

The four trends described earlier will necessitate many changes in traditional managerial policy and practice. None of them will come about easily, or by superficial modifications in conventional practice. Personnel "gadgetry" will not do the job.

Perhaps the primary change will be in a deep-seated and longstanding conception of managerial control. This conception concerns the necessity for imposing direction and limitations on the individual in order to get him to perform the work for which he is hired. It is, however, an observable characteristic of human beings that they will exercise *self*-direction and *self*-control in the service of objectives to which they are committed. These are matters of degree, of course, but I find few managements who are consciously moving in the direction of substituting self-control for externally imposed controls. The movement, if any, appears to be in the opposite direction, because this concept of self-control is erroneously associated with "soft" management.

In the recognition of this capacity of human beings to exercise self-control lies the only fruitful opportunity for industrial management to realize the full potential represented by professional resources. Creative intellectual effort of the kind upon which management will increasingly rely—in order to remain competitive—is a function of genuine commitment to objectives, under conditions that provide for a substantial degree of *self*-direction and *self*-control.

It is for this reason above all that I believe we are going to see a basic, almost revolutionary change in managerial strategy during the next two or three decades. It will not be possible in the future—because of the trends outlined earlier—for management to rely exclusively on intuition and past experience and "common sense," either in making or implementing its decisions. It will be no more possible tomorrow to manage an industrial enterprise than it is today to fly a jet aircraft "by the seat of the pants." Creative intellectual effort by a wide range of professional specialists will be as essential to tomorrow's manager as instruments and an elaborate air-traffic-control system are to today's jet pilot.

But traditional managerial strategy is primarily geared to the elaborately "programmed" and closely supervised activities of the blue-collar production worker and the clerical employee. As professional specialists become the single largest and most important class of employees in the enterprise, this traditional strategy will become hopelessly inadequate. Its greatest inadequacy will be with respect to its central concepts concerning the control of organized human effort.

Management by objectives and self-control will inevitably replace management by authority and externally imposed control. In the long run this change in strategy will affect not only professional employees but all the human resources of enterprise.

Industrial management is not entirely unaware of the necessity for change in its strategy. There is already some genuine concern over the inadequacy of current methods of control. Symptoms of underlying difficulties have been apparent for some time in industrial research laboratories (where professionals are numerous) and in engineering functions (where they are becoming so). But there is as yet little recognition that these are symptoms that will soon spread to every phase of business activity. When this recognition does occur, we will have the impetus for the development of a new managerial strategy without which the enterprise of the future will be unable to prosper.

A Philosophy of Management

I sat in a meeting a few weeks ago with a group of office department heads in a small company in Cambridge. They were considering the problems of getting people to come to work on time in the morning. What interested me was the way the conversation went in that group. One man said the solution was to install time clocks. Someone else said to take a little book and put it in a prominent place on desk at the front of each department and require anybody who came in late to sign his name in the book. The suggestions continued along the same lines. These were serious suggestions made by a group of managers who in general were doing a good job. They thought of the problem entirely in terms of the gadgets they could use to solve it. What they did not think of were the attitudes and backgrounds that they were bringing to bear on the problem. I saw in that discussion, inherent, although never expressed, feelings of this kind: "coming to work on time is something that people won't do voluntarily."

—DOUGLAS McGREGOR, *The Professional Manager*

Douglas McGregor spoken often about "management by gadgets." He felt our overemphasis on gadgets such as performance appraisals, policies, devices, formulas, incentive packages, and training often took on gadget character.

A talk presented to the Management Forum of E. I. du Pont de Nemours Co. in 1954.

Today, the number of managerial gadgets seems to have exponentially increased to keep up with technological advances. Yet, as McGregor pointed out in 1954, it is what lies behind the method or the gadget which is critically significant in determining the effectiveness. For example, if you are a manager who fundamentally mistrusts people, believes they need to be controlled to effect productivity, no matter how many times you read Stephen Covey's *Seven Habits of Highly Effective People*, attend a Tom Peters' Wow seminar or embrace the latest management study or technique, you will not be successful. The tools or techniques or thoughts run counter to your basic assumptions about people and their motivation and needs.

In this essay, "A Philosophy of Management," McGregor can serve as a guide to helping us dissect our basic assumptions and their effects in the workplace. It may also serve as a healthy reminder as we embrace the next big thing in tools, techniques, or training.

I have the impression, as I wander around the industrial scene, that there is a considerable overemphasis today on the importance of "gadgets" in the field of human relations. A variety of devices, policies, formulas, methods, and techniques are used in the attempt to solve our problems of effective management, of effective human relations. Not only is it true in industry, where we seem to be pretty gadget-minded anyway, but there are even little books on how to bring up your children, how to improve your personality, or how to become a leader. Then there are methods like job evaluation, merit rating, supervisory training, and incentive wages which also frequently take on a gadget character.

I am not opposed to methods, techniques, and formulas, but I want to make a point about them: their value and usefulness depend on the attitudes and the points of view of the people who use them. There is always something that lies behind the method which is critically significant in determining whether the method works or not.

Management through Gadgets

In Dale Carnegie's book, *How to Win Friends and Influence People,* there are some nice formulas and some nice little gadgets to use in winning friends and influencing people. But suppose we have a man who fundamentally mistrusts people, and who believes that on the whole they are rather stupid. He believes that most of them cannot really be trusted and are not particularly friendly by nature. Suppose this man sets out to apply the principles, the gadgets, that Dale Carnegie outlines. Perhaps you will agree with me that such a man will not make these methods work; in fact they may boomerang because he will use them with his tongue in his cheek. He will use them with a manner that makes it immediately apparent that they are something superficial he has taken on, that they are tools he does not really believe in. He will not win friends and influence people. On the contrary, he is more likely to make enemies by following the principles of Dale Carnegie.

I sat in a meeting a few weeks ago with a group of office department heads in a small company in Cambridge. They were considering the problem of getting people to arrive on time in the morning. What interested me was the way the conversation went in that group. One man said the solution was to install time clocks. Someone else said to take a little book and put it in a prominent place on a desk at the front of each department and require anybody who came in after the starting hour of 8:30 to sign his name in the book and the hour of his arrival at work. Another man, a little more ingenious than the rest perhaps, suggested that in his department he could arrange a turnstile at the door to the office in such a way that anybody coming in after 8:30 would ring a bell which would be heard in the whole department.

These were serious suggestions made by a group of supervisors who in general are doing a good job. They thought of that problem entirely in terms of the gadgets they could use to solve it. What they did not think of were the attitudes and the backgrounds that they were bringing to bear on the problem.

I saw in that discussion inherent, although never expressed, feelings of this kind: "Coming to work on time is something that people won't do voluntarily."

That conviction was there, or they would not have been talking about gadgets to make people come to work on time. An additional feeling that never got expressed was, "This isn't our responsibility as supervisors. Let the gadgets do it; or let the Personnel Department do it." That they should be responsible for getting their people to work on time, in a personal sense, and for doing something about it if they continued to come late, somehow did not come out. It was below the surface and was never brought out into the open.

Those attitudes and convictions about people, those conceptions of the supervisor's job, were what was responsible for the suggestions they made for solving the problem. Those attitudes certainly would have determined the use that was made of their suggestions if any of them had been adopted. I will bet my shirt that not one of the suggestions considered at that meeting could be made to work as long as those attitudes were behind what the supervisors were talking about.

Today I want to talk chiefly about a "philosophy of management." In using that word I do not want to frighten you. My point is simply this: first of all, I believe that good leadership in industry depends more than any other single thing on the manager's conception of what his job is—of what management is. Second, it depends on his convictions and on his beliefs about people. Are people inherently honest; can they be taught to be honest? Will people naturally seek responsibility under certain conditions; or do you have to fight with them to get them to accept responsibility? Will people in general break rules no matter what the rules are; or is it possible that people will live up to rules voluntarily? Convictions about matters like these make up the philosophy that lies behind the manager's job. That is what I propose to talk about.

I am not going to try to impose my philosophy on you. However, I am going to talk about some things I believe to be true about people and about the manager's job. My purpose is to get you thinking about your own philosophy. Too often we take for granted our convictions and beliefs and attitudes relating to our job as managers. Too seldom do we get them out on the table and examine them and say, "Is this realistic? Is this the way people are? Is this what my job is?" My purpose is to get you to think about your philosophy by discussing mine with you.

Management by Force

First of all, it seems to me that the job of management can be defined pretty simply. It is to achieve the objective of the organization of which management is a part. I am talking now about all management from the very top to the very bottom. Management's job is to achieve the objective of the enterprise, and that purpose in our economy today may likewise be fairly simply stated: it is the production and sales of goods or services at a profit. That is what industrial enterprises exist for, and management is hired to accomplish that purpose.

The organization that management works with consists of plant, equipment, materials, machines, and people. To integrate all of those things, to organize them in such a way that the objective of the organization is achieved, is the job of management. In earlier days, management tended to treat plant, equipment, materials, and people without differentiating between them. We had what the economists now refer to as the "commodity theory of labor." This was the idea that the labor of people who worked for the enterprise could be bought and sold in the same way as the materials that were used. Various managements, small and large, treated people exactly that way. They did not differentiate between the machine and the person as far as managerial tactics were concerned.

Unfortunately, for management at any rate, it did not work too well. People were not docile, they were not as passive as the machinery in relation to management's wishes. If you get a machine properly set up, you push a button and the machine operates; it does not talk back to you or resist you.

Initially, in the early days after the Industrial Revolution, people were pretty docile. However, as the standard of living got a little higher, and people got a greater sense of dignity and personal responsibility, they began to get active themselves. Frequently, management found that the people were interfering with management's task of achieving the organizational objective through restriction of output or failure to live up to rules, by not doing what they were told, and sometimes through strikes and open rebellion of one kind or another. Some managements were faced with that kind of problem and for the first time had to differentiate between the material and human aspects of the organization.

Operating from the point of view that their job was to get the organization's purpose achieved through manipulating the ingredients, some managements simply said, "Well, if people won't be docile, we'll make them." The philosophy behind the tactics of such a management was, essentially, "Be strong, be tough, break down resistance and antagonism, and get the job done that way." The trick is to make people afraid through fear of unemployment. Even today, we find among some managements traces of that feeling. Some managers say, "I wish, fundamentally, that we could have a pretty severe depression again, because in a depression, when there are a lot more people than there are jobs, people do what they are told. They don't stand up on their hind legs and sneer at the boss. They are not insubordinate; they don't assert themselves the way they do when there is lots of work. It would be nice if we had a depression so we, management, could get in the driver's seat."

The difficulty with a philosophy of management that demands docile people and that argues, "if they are not docile we must make them become docile," is simply that it does not work, because it ignores a fundamental point that most of us know about human behavior. Psychologists dress this point up in fancy terms. They talk about the "frustration-aggression hypothesis." The idea is simply this: it is a primitive, natural, normal human reaction when we are frustrated—when we are blocked in attempting to achieve satisfaction of our needs—to kick back, to fight. You see it in the small child who, when reprimanded by papa, tends naturally to kick papa in the shins. Of course, the child learns quickly that this does not work. He discovers that it means more frustration. The child may revert to ways of expressing his aggression toward papa that are a little more subtle, but they accomplish the same purpose.

You come home some night tired and worn out. The things you want above all else are a cool drink and your paper and slippers for a half hour of relaxation before dinner. Little Johnnie, aged four or five, is around waiting to play baseball. You tell him, "Sorry, but I don't feel like baseball tonight; run and play somewhere else for a half hour while I read my paper." Then you get the drink out and get all settled comfortably with the paper.

Johnnie is playing around the room, bouncing his ball and a little unhappy. Of course, he does not say anything. Now it just happens—and I'm sure Johnnie did not intend it—but it does happen that Johnnie's ball bounces your way and tips over your drink!

There are all kinds of ways—some of them are not even conscious—in which we express our aggression when we are frustrated. Restriction of output, various kinds of "sabotage," waste, spoilage, and many other things happen on the job. Frequently these are simply symptoms, but yet they are an expression of people's reactions to feelings of frustration. Sometimes people are not even aware that they are being aggressive, but management has generally found out that these reactions to frustration defeat management's own purpose in one way or the other.

So, attempting to make people be docile, I believe, is an unrealistic approach. It is a philosophy that fundamentally will not work.

The Philosophy of Paternalism

Some managements made an altogether different attack on this problem. They said in effect, "Be good. If you're good, people out of loyalty and gratitude will do what you want them to do." Notice that the notion of docility is still there. The idea is that management has a job to do: to accomplish the organization's purpose through people. It can only accomplish that purpose if people do what they are told—if they are docile and accept orders.

The first group we talked about simply said, "If they won't, make them do it." The second group thought about it another way. The idea was, "Be good to them and they will do what you want them to." Out of this second group stems the whole philosophy of paternalism with which many of us are familiar.

Unfortunately, this philosophy has not worked too well either. When you simply give people things—which is what this philosophy promotes—it follows that they want more things: "Here is a lovely Santa Claus, who makes everything possible for me and gives me a lot of things I want. My attitude toward that Santa Claus is, come around again with your pack. If he doesn't, I'm frustrated by the fact that he hasn't given me some more."

People do not in general give their loyalties or their efforts out of gratitude; in fact, it makes them feel a little uncomfortable to be put in that dependent position. We have had several instances across the country of severe strikes and violent upheavals in companies that have been noted for their excessive paternalism. Employees who, to all intents and purposes, have everything, stand up in rebellion and say, "We don't want to be given things." Behind that is a certain feeling, perhaps, that it lowers their sense of importance to have somebody else decide what is good for them.

There is one other approach that has been characteristic of some managements. This approach is a compromise between the other two. It seems to me that it emerged during the last war, when management realized that a lot of tactics that had been used in the past did not seem to be working too well. Employees were pretty uppity and very hard to handle, particularly if the attempt was to make them docile. That compromise was essentially this: "Be firm, but fair; give them the wages and the benefits to which they are entitled, in terms of the community and the place in which you operate. Don't be tough, don't try to make them do what you tell them, but be firm. Draw a line somewhere and don't move beyond that line."

I do not believe that any company that has followed this philosophy will say it is the final answer to our problems of human relations. The reason it does not work too well is that it is a compromise between two fundamentally unworkable principles. Neither the "be good" nor the "be tough" philosophy will in itself accomplish the job. When you simply take part of each of them, you have not come up with any real answer to the problem.

Cooperation for Organizational Objectives

My belief is that we must shift our frame of reference, our way of looking at management's problems, in order to find even partial answers to the difficulties I have been describing. From my point of view, the key to the difficulty with the traditional philosophy of management lies in the notion of the necessity for docility—the notion that if people would only do what they were told we could get our job done well. Quite frankly, I do not believe that people will ever do what they are told. I believe that managements that try to approach their job in that frame of mind are inevitably going to get frustrated.

Let us start again by saying that management's job is to get the organizational objective achieved: the production and sale of goods at a profit. But let us take a little different attitude. We do not regard people as a commodity now; we do not ask them to be docile. We say that management's task is to get people's cooperation, to create the conditions under which people will willingly and voluntarily work toward organizational objectives.

That may sound like an idealistic goal. However, if we could get even a majority of the people in an organization to work toward organizational objectives because they wanted to, management's job would be a very different job. I do not argue that this can be achieved today, tomorrow, or ten years from now; but I do argue that, if this is the goal toward which management directs its thinking, management will approach the day-to-day job in a very different way than if the goal is "Make them do what they are told," or "Be good, and then they will do what they are told." It is a fundamentally different slant on management's job.

What are some of the conditions that management could create, or some of the problems that management could help to solve, if it took upon itself that task? It does not make any difference whether you are a supervisor or at the first level, a manager in the middle, or the president on the top. The problem is to do your part of accomplishing the organizational objective. Let us suppose now that your attitude and philosophy are: "How can I get people voluntarily to want to work together toward the organization's objectives?"

In a way, what I am talking of is a little like the problem that an engineer faces when he is going to design a machine. He knows in advance the things he wants the machine to accomplish. Then, if he uses the right materials and puts them together in the right way, with enough skill on his part, he will eventually get a machine that works. Of course, that machine never works as well as the ideal of physical theory might indicate, because we always have friction (among other things) to cope with. However, we can approach the ideal. The same thing is true in designing a human organization. We may never get to the ideal, but if we have the ideal in mind we can hope at least to approach it.

I should like to make three or four points that seem to me to be pertinent if one adopts this different philosophy of attempting to get voluntary cooperation as a manager. The first is this rather simple but fundamental notion about human behavior: all human behavior is directed toward the satisfaction of needs. Life is a struggle for need satisfaction, extending from birth 'til death. In fact, when we cease trying to satisfy our needs, we *are* dead. Of all the kinds of needs, there are three that are crucially important to us as managers working with people in industry. First, there are the physical needs for such things as food, shelter, clothing, air, elimination, exercise, rest, and all of the biological necessities of the organism. They are obvious and they are important, of course.

Second, there is a cluster of needs that I like to call social. These grow out of the fact that we live in a highly interdependent society in which we no longer do things for ourselves. We no longer build our own houses, or make our own clothes, or grow our own food. We are dependent, all of us, on other people for getting our needs satisfied, and therefore it is inevitable that we should develop needs of a social sort. There is the need for companionship, the need for status among one's fellows, the desire to be regarded in the eyes of our associates as an acceptable person, and so on. These social needs work both ways—they are not only a "taking-in affair," but also a "giving-out affair." People get real enjoyment from behavior that is directed toward the group, and in helping the group to achieve its goals.

Finally, there is a group that I call egoistic needs, the needs that relate to the person himself. Such things as the need for achievement—to accomplish something, to solve a difficult task and be able to pat yourself on the chest and say, "I did that." Then there are the needs for knowledge, for creativity, for recognition and prestige in other people's eyes.

Need Satisfactions on the Job

These physical, social, and egoistic needs are the things that people are striving to satisfy throughout their lives, whether they may be on the job or off the job. The problem management has, if it is going to adopt this philosophy of voluntary cooperation, is to find ways in which behavior directed toward organizational purposes will provide satisfaction of such needs as these. When we make that explicit, and when we start to examine it, we will find that management has frequently missed some opportunities.

First and fundamentally, unless people believe down deep inside themselves that they can get their needs satisfied from the job to a reasonable degree, then they are not going to be willing to work for us voluntarily. They may do it out of fear, but not voluntarily. That notion of a kind of emotional security, or confidence that the job will provide opportunities for need satisfaction, is crucial in creating cooperation.

There is where the boss comes in, because it is the boss who tends to control those opportunities for need satisfaction. The boss controls wages and promotions. He controls the opportunity to "swing your cat a little bit" on your own job, to be creative, to solve problems, and to get knowledge. I must have a genuine confidence that he is going to give me the best break he can so that I can get my needs satisfied. Therefore, the first requirement is a basic confidence on the part of people in their managers. That is the foundation, and without it you have nothing.

The second point is a little less obvious, but I think it is equally important. The people that work for us spend about a third of their waking lives on the job. Consider how much in the way of real need satisfaction they get in the work situation itself, on the job. We pay them wages, but they cannot spend their wages at work; they have to go somewhere else to get that need satisfaction. We give them vacations, but they cannot enjoy their vacations at work. We give them pensions, but they cannot get that satisfaction while they work; they must retire and leave the job. As a matter of fact, when you go down the list of things that we provide people as means for need satisfaction from working, practically all of them are things that they can utilize for satisfaction only when they leave the job and go somewhere else.

Unless the job itself can be satisfying, unless there are opportunities right in the work situation to get fun out of working, we will never get people to direct their efforts voluntarily towards organizational goals. In fact, the reverse happens. Work becomes a kind of punishment they undergo in order to get those things they require for need satisfaction after they leave the job.

You, as management, frequently underestimate the importance of this problem for the people who work for you. Because of being in the management group, you automatically get a greater degree of need satisfaction in work itself. You have greater freedom, more opportunities for social satisfaction, more opportunities for achievement, for acquiring additional knowledge, for being creative. All of the things that can provide satisfaction at work are more available to you than they are to the fellow on the bottom. Even there, I think there is a gradient as one moves up the organizational ladder from the bottom to the top. The opportunities for having your work be fun, be enjoyable, be satisfying, get greater the higher up the line you go.

The third thought (the first was confidence, the second was on-the-job satisfaction) relates to a psychological law. Once again, I think you will recognize it in common-sense terms: behavior that leads to punishment or to lack of satisfaction tends to drop out. We call this the law of effect. Stop and examine for a moment how much of the behavior of the people working for you that results in need satisfaction for them is behavior directed toward organizational goals. The problem is to see to it that behavior that is directed toward organizational goals is satisfying to people, and that it is satisfying in proportion to the effort they put out toward organizational goals.

Are we set up that way? Do we run our departments that way? Well, consider wages and salaries. Is the person paid in general in such a fashion that the harder he works for the organization the more he gets? Perhaps so, in the long run through promotions and pay increases. That depends a lot on how the manager runs the wage-administration program. Does he really reward effort toward organizational purposes, or does he reward the employee who plays up to him, who is careful to consider the boss' prejudices? Does the boss play favorites? If he does, he is not rewarding behavior toward organizational goals.

In many instances, as I see the thing operate (and this is particularly true at the hourly wage level), the way you collect your day's wages is to stay employed. That's all. If you can keep from being fired, you get your wages. That forces the individual to the minimum of performance that he can get by with. The average worker today does not direct his energy toward organizational goals with the idea that if he does he can get promoted, because statistically he knows that his chances of promotion are pretty small. Some people are motivated that way; the great mass of people are not. Consequently, if we want their genuine cooperation, we must make sure that the need satisfaction we offer cannot be obtained merely by the minimum effort that enables them to stay employed.

When we turn to the other benefits we offer, the picture is even clearer. How do you get your vacation pay? How do you get your pension? How do you get your holidays? How do you get your insurance benefits? By working harder for the organization and helping to achieve organizational goals? No, not a bit of it. So long as you are employed—if you keep from being fired—you will get them, just like death and taxes. Somewhere along the line we have to find ways (and I do not think they will be solely in the form of money returns) to see to it that people get genuine satisfaction out of directing their efforts toward organizational goals.

Through the utilization of ideas like the principle of consultative supervision, our subordinates can get the feeling of increased dignity, of achievement, of prestige, of social satisfaction. Those are important ways in which people can get satisfaction by working toward organizational goals. However, you, as managers, must provide those opportunities; they will not just happen.

One other point. There are big differences in the kinds of opportunities that can be provided for people to obtain need satisfaction. It is relatively easy to provide means (chiefly in the form of money) for need satisfaction—at least until the supply is exhausted. You cannot, however, provide people with a sense of achievement, or with knowledge, or with prestige. You can provide *opportunities* for them to obtain these satisfactions through efforts directed toward organization goals. What is even more important, the *supply of such opportunities*— unlike the supply of money—*is unlimited*.

This philosophy of management is not an easy one to practice. It offers, nevertheless, a challenge to all of us. It has one important virtue: it does not require the impossible task of making human beings docile, of creating conditions in which they will do what they are told without questions or resistance. Management in the past has tried to do the impossible, partly because of a faulty conception of human behavior and human motivation. Today we can correct that error if we will.

Chairman Mac
by Warren Bennis

Douglas McGregor was an epochal figure in his own time, and remains one, for that matter. He created a "new taste" across the entire field of management and the newer field of organizational behavior. One can agree or disagree with his writings, but they are always there as something to shoot for or at, depending on one's viewpoint. All of us who live and work in large, organized settings—practitioners and scholars alike—sing his exultant chants, or lament their popularity, or question their validity. Just as every economist, knowingly or not, pays his dues to Keynes, we are all, one way or another, McGregorian.

Douglas McGregor was my teach, colleague, boss and friend. We met at a point in my life—they don't happen so frequently as one grows older—when I was extra vulnerable to what nowadays is called a "role model." I was fresh out of the Army, age 22, and restarting at Antioch College as a freshman during the time when he was its president. His reputation had been secured through a clutch of magazine articles and his teaching at the Massachusetts Institute of Technology, where he headed the Industrial Relations Section.

I mention this at the outset—although our friendship is well-known—to warn the reader that I am not "your neutral critic" (if,

Reprinted with permission of the *Harvard Business Review*. Every so often, someone encapsulates a timely idea in such striking wording that the idea quickly penetrates the general consciousness. Such is the case with "Theory X" and "Theory Y." The ideas they represent were not new when Douglas McGregor established these twin "theories," but he labeled them and around them articulated a philosophy with which anyone who deals with people in organizations must come to terms. In this article, a colleague and friend of the late social scientist uses McGregor's "classic" HBR article (see page 133) as a springboard for a retrospective on the impact of his work and life. Mr. Bennis is President of the University of Cincinnati. Formerly, he was a professor at M.I.T. and a teacher and administrator at the State University of New York at Buffalo. He coedited two posthumous collections of McGregor's writings, *Leadership and Motivation* and *The Professional Manager*. Among the books he has written in his own right are *Interpersonal Dynamics, Changing Organizations*, and *The Temporary Society*. His latest book, *Who Sank the Yellow Submarine?*—dealing with the plight of American universities—will be published late in 1972.

indeed, any critic is totally neutral; one's biases are always there, tacit perhaps, but easily discerned, the way a batter can detect a pitcher's curves). Despite all that, I believe I can be detached—if not "objective"—and even critical toward one who has meant so much to me personally. McGregor possessed a craggy tentativeness, a lust for exploration, and an irresistible charm that was hard to cope with, if one had reason to fight it. But what made me admire him so much at the time—although I never verbalized it to myself until much later, when we became "grown-up" friends during our years together at M.I.T.— was the fact that he pretty much embodied (or tried to) the theories he wrote about.

When he was unable to exemplify that ideal, for whatever reasons, he felt sick or guilty or, usually, both. He fretted a lot about that, and I am certain that the deep lines in his face, the so-called "worry lines," were gouged more deeply because of that persistent fear, guilt feeling, or whatever. I am also convinced that these occasional and quite understandable contradictions between his writings and his personal life were a partial cause of his premature death in 1964, at the age of 58.

That Famous 'Y'

His work, like his personality, was all of a piece. Nothing he wrote failed to reflect, in one way or another, his later-to-be-developed trademark now immortalized by the simple initial "Y."

His famous "Theory Y" speech was delivered at the Fifth Anniversary Convocation of M.I.T.'s Alfred P. Sloan School of Management in April 1957. "The Human Side of Enterprise" was the title of the speech, and it was under that title that McGregor published his first book in 1960.[1] He adapted the important HBR article, "An Uneasy Look at Performance Appraisal," as a chapter in it. The book continues to do well 12 years after publication; the last time I saw the publisher's sales graphs, its sales were running at about 30,000 copies a year.

---

[1] New York, McGraw-Hill.

What did McGregor say to captivate the managerial public he was addressing? Basically, he postulated a new theory of man (partly borrowed from the psychological theorists of "self-actualization," especially Abraham Maslow), a new theory of power, and a new set of values that would guide the spirit of the industrial workplace. They can be summed up under his useful dichotomy, Theory X and Theory Y.

Theory X represents a series of propositions about what McGregor felt was the conventional conception of management's task in harnessing human energy to organizational requirements. In the speech he listed them this way:

- "Management is responsible for organizing the elements of productive enterprise—money, materials, equipment, people—in the interest of economic ends.
- "With respect to people, this is a process of directing their efforts, motivating them, controlling their actions, modifying their behavior to fit the needs of the organization.
- "Without this active intervention by management, people would be passive—even resistant—to organizational needs.
- "The average man is by nature indolent—he works as little as possible.
- "He lacks ambition, dislikes responsibility, prefers to be led.
- "He is inherently self-centered, indifferent to organizational needs.
- "He is by nature resistant to change.
- "He is gullible, not very bright, the ready dupe of the charlatan and the demagogue."

McGregor believed that conventional organizational structures, practices, and managerial policies reflect and reinforce these assumptions.

Now that I have quoted the elements of Theory X, I realize that Theory X is alive and living in most of our institutions—regardless of how intellectually acceptable Theory Y is or how spectacular the book sales are. It is not only alive in our industrial world, but active in the assumptions behind advertising campaigns, political campaigns, educational practices, and the management of welfare and health institutions. Why did I once think it was not?

In his speech, McGregor presented Theory Y, using another set of propositions:

- "People are *not* by nature passive or resistant to organizational needs. They have become so as a result of experience in organizations.
- "The motivation, the potential for development, the capacity for assuming responsibility, the readiness to direct behavior toward organizational goals are all present in people. Management does not put them there. It is a responsibility of management to make it possible for people to recognize and develop these human characteristics for themselves.
- "The essential task of management is to arrange organizational conditions and methods of operation so that people can achieve their own goals *best* by directing *their own* efforts toward organizational objectives."

Furthermore, he said, "This is a process primarily of creating opportunities, releasing potential, removing obstacles, encouraging growth, providing guidance. It is what Peter Drucker has called 'management by objectives' in contrast to 'management by control.'"

"An Uneasy Look at Performance Appraisal" is studded with Theory Y assumptions—though it was published long before that phrase was immortalized. It doesn't take an organizational theorist to spot them; they fairly leap out at you. Consider:

- "Resistance to conventional appraisal programs is eminently sound. It reflects an unwillingness to treat human beings like physical objects. The needs of the organization are obviously important, but when they come into conflict with our convictions about the worth and the dignity of the human personality, one or the other must give."

- "[The subordinate] is no longer a pawn in a chess game called management development."
- "Effective development of managers does not include coercing them (no matter how benevolently) into acceptance of the goals of the enterprise, not does it mean manipulating their behavior to suit organizational needs. Rather, it calls for creating a relationship within which a man can take responsibility for developing his own potentialities, plan for himself, and learn from putting his plans into action. In the process he can gain a genuine sense of satisfaction, for he is utilizing his own capabilities to achieve simultaneously both his objectives and those of the organization."

All the themes that informed his earlier work and those that culminated in *The Human Side of Enterprise* are there:

- Active participation by all involved.
- A transcending concern with individual dignity, worth, and growth.
- Reexamination and resolution of the conflict between individual needs and organizational goals, through effective interpersonal relationships between superiors and subordinates.
- A concept of influence that relies not on coercion, compromise, evasion or avoidance, pseudosupport, or bargaining, but on openness, confrontation, and "working through" differences.
- A belief that human growth is self-generated and furthered by an environment of trust, feedback, and authentic human relationships.

The employee must take the responsibility for his own growth. McGregor would not tolerate "pseudogrowth" forced on the individual by the overzealous superior who manipulates, no matter how well intentioned he is, or by a sadist who uses fear as a crutch to hide his own fears. Growth is organic, natural. The best a leader can do is understand the conditions creating a climate of growth and do his best to irrigate. The leader intervenes only rarely—and at great risk.

I want to underline something now that I passed over too quickly before. Theory Y (and X, for that matter) does not necessarily reflect attributes of the "subordinate"—a term McGregor often used, which lends a certain rustic, archaic tone to the article—but constitutes a set of assumptions held by the manager (or "superior") toward his workers. Theory X or Theory Y is the manager's construct or hypothesis about human behavior; or to be somewhat fancier, if not more precise, it is part of his "cosmology," his existential core. McGregor believed that the manager's constructs of motivation—not gleaned from books, but drawn from the library of life—create the conditions whereby the subordinates' behavior is or may be Y-ish or X-ish. Perhaps that is why McGregor found the concept of the "self-fulfilling prophecy" so fetching and useful.

Expectations about the "the other" (a ubiquitous and important, if somewhat shadowy, figure in most of the social sciences) to a large extent determine the appropriate behavioral response. In short, treat workers as if they care, have integrity, and want to be committed to the organization and work hard toward its goals. And, the wonder of it is, they do. Or most of them do.

Disciples and Critics

McGregor's writings, especially after the enthusiastic reception of *The Human Side of Enterprise,* facilitated—if not directly influenced—a number of related developments in the practice of management. The application of T-groups (sensitivity training and so forth) to actual, on-line, real-life organizations began in earnest in the late 1950s and has continued at an accelerated rate to the present. McGregor's work provided the badly needed theory that attempted to translate a "small group" model of change—basically an interpersonal one—from a laboratory situation, distant in time and space from the sweaty and plebeian day-to-day life of the real world, to intact, functioning organizations. The work of Likert, Haire, Clark, Blake and Mouton, Argyris, Schein, Leavitt, Shepard, Beckhard, and so many others owes in large part its acceptance and development to McGregor's writings.

The newer field of organizational development, nowadays referred to as "OD," emerged from this tradition and has since matured into

an important area of theory, research, and practice. One example of
the practical consequences of this development is the establishment of
new departments and corporate vice presidents of OD. These departments and executives take as their chief responsibility the examination and promotion of work environments that facilititate Theory Y
responses.

Douglas McGregor's writings attracted devoted disciples and devoted critics. They were bound to, for any new and useful idea always
bootlegs in prescriptive and moral imperatives that stand at an angle to
conventions and practices. Of course, there were some who criticized
his work because they detected in it (quite correctly) a style of behavior
antithetical to their own value systems.

Our attitudes about leadership and followership are not exclusively
rational or cognitive. They go to the very core of our character. One can
change *style*, I suppose—how easily I am not certain, although politi-
cians seem to carry it off almost as well as good actors. But *character?*

Our conceptions of leadership are formed relatively early in life.
They are based on family, church, and school experiences, so that we
"know in our hearts" what's right (and wrong) about leadership behavior. Consequently, it is far easier to search for fallacies in a theory or
find a lack of scientific confirmation or empirical validity than it is to
question one's basic values or self-concept.

The imagery of leadership in American society (and most others,
for that matter) is forged from a long heritage of folklore, fables, myths,
ritual, and literature about heroes: Moses, Gary Cooper out of "High
Noon," Lawrence of Arabia, Henry Ford, Andrew Carnegie, "Boss"
Kettering, and the lonely conquistador whether in science (Newton
and Darwin) or the practical arts (Edison and Columbus).

These heroes are courageous, "self-made," without friends or colleagues, swashbuckling, and single-handedly triumphing over great odds.
These primal types are as natural and automatic to us as breathing.

How could a Theory Y manager run a railroad? How could a
leader *listen* so much without appearing passive, weak, or permissive? It
sounds like a cream-puff, "oh-you-kid" kind of leadership style. The

leader should lead, damn it! It's performance, not buddy-buddy non-sense, that counts. Anyway, nice guys finish last. How could a philosophy of management work that gives away the prerogatives of decision making to subordinates? That sounds suspiciously like communism.

Those aren't concocted criticisms; they represent only a mild sampling of typical responses. The one about communism is (or used to be) frequently expressed, and is undoubtedly the least relevant to McGregor's argument. McGregor steadfastly held to the accountability and responsibility of the formal organization's leadership. "Power equalization," a term applied to Theory Y by a few thoughtful critics, just doesn't hold water. McGregor, at least, never hinted or implied any surrender of power.

Indeed, he argued that a trusting, open, and honest superior-subordinate relationship adds to, rather than subtracts from, the superior's ability to influence his subordinate. (Incidentally, this also means that it adds to the subordinate's ability to influence his superior.)

Cautionary Notes

Two justifiable criticisms of McGregor's work come to mind. They are not especially new, nor were they unknown to him. We discussed them a number of times, though I must confess that one of the two never was clearly answered. That one has to do with the burden assumed by the boss. The other concerns application of Theory Y in an increasingly complex world.

How to satisfy the boss's needs? The poet W.H. Auden once wrote that every genius possesses an "essential error," some skewed distortion of reality that informs his work. In McGregor, the essential error can be detected throughout his work, although, like "invisible weaving," it may not be discernible at the surface.

It is directly related to his conception of Theory Y leadership. What is a Theory Y leader really like, according to McGregor's description (and enshrinement) of him? He is caring, protective, a wise helper-counselor.

He rarely intervenes except when asked or when absolutely necessary. He is a perceptive human ecologist, adjusting dials and cultivating the perfect organizational climate so that his labors, unsung and unnoticed, create Pygmalion-like transformations in his charges.

The success or failure of his subordinates is *his* responsibility, really, despite McGregor's claim that individual growth is a function of the individual himself. For, after all, the boss, like the mother who uses Dr. Spock's books (McGregor and Spock have a lot in common), is held responsible for the nurture and development of his employees (offspring). Whether they develop, succeed, and "actualize" is his burden.

But in this human equation, where and when do the boss's needs, growth, defenses, distortions, "hang-ups," disappointments, narcissism, sufferings come into play? Has he been so beautifully sensitized or superanalyzed that he actually has no needs—or, if he does, will not press them on others? Is it enough to play a Pygmalion game in the factory? Is it enough to experience the epiphany of successive, vicarious parental triumphs?

I wonder whether the Theory Y leader can trust the capacity, resources, or maturity of underlings to understand, let alone cope with, his full range as a person. Can he freely express his imperfections and learn from his employees (as I think he should be able to) so that he can realize his full human potential?

Theory Y leadership doesn't strike me as fully human. For where does it allow anger, destructiveness, inconsistency, or playfulness? What does it say about people (employees) who are competent loners, incorrigible weaklings, liars, villains, or those Thurber-like characters who simply don't want to be helped, counseled, and nurtured? What does it say about those who, for whatever reason, want to remain distant from authority figures? Are they all Portnoys?

I wonder whether employees may not feel "infantalized" through behavior that is truly Christ-like and that ultimately reflects not only the leader's lack of trust in his charges but also a more important and more subtle lack of trust in himself.

In "An Uneasy Look at Performance Appraisal," in other writings, and in lectures, McGregor fumed against "playing God." Perhaps the old-fashioned, free-wheeling autocrat was. But what does it mean to sublimate one's own achievements and recognition in the service of the inchoate and eminently protean subordinate? White man's burden— that's what it means to me. I wonder what that burden does to the human psyche.

I wonder, too, what life would be like on a planet populated by Theory Y leaders. On balance, it would probably be an improvement. But the price for those who seek this style of influence should be posted for all to see.

Environmental void: The second of my criticisms has been voiced by many others and was fully recognized by McGregor. Indeed, at the time of his death he was finishing a book, *The Professional Manager*, which took into account many, though not all, of these shortcomings.

The criticism goes this way: McGregor's theory of organization depends on a psychologically determined set of superior-subordinate relationships operating in an environmental void. There are no technological factors, norms, or groups, nor are there economic, cultural, legal, or political impositions. Nor does the theory fully take into account changing world conditions, such as educational advancements, pollution, conflict, and population growth, that bring strong environmental forces to bear on the micro-organization.

The organizational environment is becoming more active, turbulent, spastic, and consequential. Organizational goals, to take just one example, cannot be determined solely by the subordinate (in collaboration with his superior, to be sure) because they are nowadays more than ever challenged and revised by shareholders, consumer advocates, taxpayers, and many other noisy and incessantly demanding constituencies.

Without elaborating the point, I can say that, in addition to the forces within the organization which McGregor's work never fully recognized or reckoned with, increasingly powerful external forces are registering their impact on decision making. Constituents, political bodies, judicial overkill, foreign relations and trade, and the mass media are a few.

So perhaps the growth of organizational complexity and the increased interdependency of various institutions make McGregor's image of the superior-subordinate relationship as moot as an earlier image of the educational process has become. I am referring to Mark Hopkins on one end of a log and a student on the other. It's a swift stream, with lots of surprises and turbulence still ahead. Possibly we ought to worry about the viability of the very idea of two persons on a log.

Marks of Genius

Criticizing McGregor helps me to remember his genius, far more than the panegyrics that I and others have lavished on the man and his works. Near the beginning of this article I implied that we have internalized his ideas and concepts. We take them for granted, forgetting his contribution in the process. McGregor helped me invent my very first aphorism: "The good parent, the good teacher, and the good consultant all share one thing in common: they always give birth to orphans." He was that inspirational a teacher.

He was a genius, not necessarily for the originality of his ideas, which were often "in the air" or developed by similarly creative spirits. He was a genius because he had clarity of mind, a rare empathy for the manager, and a flair for the right metaphor that established a new idea.

Ideas are always invented before their founders hit on them. There must have been an "identity crisis" before Erikson coined the phrase. Theory X and Theory Y certainly existed before McGregor. But he named them, called them. The old joke about the umpire in the last half of the last inning in the last and determining game of the World Series comes to mind. The score is tied, the bases are loaded, two are out, and the batter has a 3-2 count. The ball is pitched and the umpire hesitates. The batter turns around angrily and shouts: "Well, what the hell is it?" And the umpire replies: "It ain't nothing till I call it!"

"Calling it" in science or in the world of practice requires not only those other remarkable attributes of McGregor, but that important and difficult element, courage. He had that, too,—in abundance.

In 1950, McGregor wrote:

"Out of all this has come the first clear recognition of an inescapable fact: we cannot successfully force people to work for management's objectives. The ancient conception that people do the work of the world only if they are forced to do so by threats or intimidation, or by the camouflaged authoritarian methods of paternalism, has been suffering from a lingering fatal illness for a quarter of a century. I venture the guess that it will be dead in another decade."[2]

He was characteristically optimistic about the death of authoritarianism, but he was unerring, as usual, in putting his finger on the right issue at the right time. He might have helped, had he lived, to bring it about a lot sooner.

---

[2] Personal communication quoted in my book, *Organization Development* (Reading, Massachusetts, Addison-Wesley, 1969), p. 76.

An Uneasy Look at Performance Appraisal

Performance appraisal within management ranks has become standard practice in many companies during the past 20 years and is currently being adopted by many others, often as an important feature of management development programs. The more the method is used, the more uneasy I grow over the unstated assumptions which lie behind it. Moreover, with some searching, I find that a number of people both in education and in industry share my misgivings. This article, therefore, has two purposes:

1. To examine the conventional performance appraisal plan which requires the manager to pass judgment on the personal worth of subordinates.
2. To describe an alternative which places on the subordinate the primary responsibility for establishing performance goals and appraising progress toward them.

"Managers are uncomfortable when they are put in the position of 'playing God,'" Douglas McGregor wrote in explaining their resistance to undertaking the conventional kind of appraisal of employee performance. Instead, he advocated an approach in which the subordinate establishes personal short-term goals and evaluates his performance himself. As a consequence, interviews with his manager concentrate on the employee's strengths, rather than his shortcomings, and tend less to digress into personalities. This article is as pertinent today as when it first appeared in the May-June 1957 issue of HBR. That its ideas are not as fresh now is testimony to the wide acceptance of McGregor's belief in encouraging individuals to develop their potentialities in the organizational setting. In 1957 he had not yet articulated his famous concepts of Theory X and Theory Y, although, as Warren G. Bennis points out in the retrospective commentary on McGregor that follows, the ideas behind them are present in this "HBR Classic."

At the time this article was written, McGregor was Professor of Management at the School of Industrial Management, Massachusetts Institute of Technology. Previously, he had been active in the field of industrial relations and had been President of Antioch College. He died in 1964.

Current Programs

Formal performance appraisal plans are designed to met three needs, one for the organization and two for the individual:

1. They provide systematic judgments to back up salary increases, promotions, transfers, and sometimes demotions or terminations.
2. They are a means of telling a subordinate how he is doing, and suggesting needed changes in his behavior, attitudes, skills, or job knowledge; they let him know "where he stands" with the boss.
3. They also are being increasingly used as a basis for the coaching and counseling of the individual by the superior.

Problem of Resistance

Personnel administrators are aware that appraisal programs tend to run into resistance from the managers who are expected to administer them. Even managers who admit the necessity of such programs frequently balk at the process—especially the interview part. As a result, some companies do not communicate appraisal results to the individual, despite the general conviction that the subordinate has a right to know his superior's opinion so he can correct his weaknesses.

The boss's resistance is usually attributed to the following causes:

- A normal dislike of criticizing a subordinate (and perhaps having to argue about it).
- Lack of skill needed to handle the interviews.
- Dislike of a new procedure with its accompanying changes in ways of operating.
- Mistrust of the validity of the appraisal instrument.

To meet this problem, formal controls—scheduling, reminders, and so on—are often instituted. It is common experience that without them fewer than half the appraisal interviews are actually held. But even controls do not necessarily work. Thus:

In one company with a well-planned and carefully administered appraisal program, an opinion poll included two questions regarding appraisals. More than 90% of those answering the questionnaire approved the idea of appraisals. They wanted to know how they stood. Some 40% went on to say that they had never had the experience of being told—yet the files showed that over four-fifths of them had signed a form testifying that they had been through an appraisal interview, some of them several times!

The respondents had no reason to lie, nor was there the slightest supposition that their superiors had committed forgery. The probable explanation is that the superiors, being basically resistant to the plan, had conducted the interviews in such a perfunctory manner that many subordinates did not realize what was going on.

Training programs designed to teach the skills of appraising and interviewing do help, but they seldom eliminate managerial resistance entirely. The difficulties connected with "negative appraisals" remain a source of genuine concern. There is always some discomfort involved in telling a subordinate he is not doing well. The individual who is "coasting" during the few years prior to retirement after serving his company competently for many years presents a special dilemma to the boss who is preparing to interview him.

Nor does a shift to a form of group appraisal solve the problem. Though the group method tends to have greater validity and, properly administered, can equalize varying standards of judgment, it does not ease the difficulty inherent in the interview. In fact, the superior's discomfort is often intensified when he must base his interview on the results of a *group* discussion of the subordinate's worth. Even if the final judgments have been his, he is not free to discuss the things said by others which may have influenced him.

The Underlying Cause

What should we think about a method—however valuable for meeting organizational needs—which produces such results in a wide range of companies with a variety of appraisal plans? The problem is one that cannot be dismissed lightly.

Perhaps this intuitive managerial reaction to conventional performance appraisal plans shows a deep but unrecognized wisdom. In my view, it does not reflect anything so simple as resistance to change, or dislike for personnel technique, or lack of skill, or mistrust for rating scales. Rather, managers seem to be expressing real misgivings, which they find difficult to put into words. This could be the underlying cause:

The conventional approach, unless handled with consummate skill and delicacy, constitutes something dangerously close to a violation of the integrity of the personality. Managers are uncomfortable when they are put in the position of "playing God." The respect we hold for the inherent value of the individual leaves us distressed when we must take responsibility for judging the personal worth of a fellow man. Yet the conventional approach to performance appraisal forces us not only to make such judgments and to see them acted upon but also to communicate them to those we have judged. Small wonder we resist!

The modern emphasis upon the manager as a leader who strives to *help* his subordinates achieve both their own and the company's objectives is hardly consistent with the judicial role demanded by most appraisal plans. If the manager must put on his judicial hat occasionally, he does it reluctantly and with understandable qualms. Under such conditions, it is unlikely that the subordinate will be any happier with the results than will the boss. It will not be surprising, either, if he fails to recognize that he has been told where he stands.

Of course, managers cannot escape making judgments about subordinates. Without such evaluations, salary and promotion policies cannot be administered sensibly. But are subordinates like products on an assembly line, to be accepted or rejected as a result of an inspection process? The inspection process may be made more objective or more accurate through research on the appraisal instrument, through training of the "inspectors," or through introducing group appraisal; the subordinate may be "reworked" by coaching or counseling before the final decision to accept or reject him; but as far as the assumptions of the conventional appraisal process are concerned, we still have what is practically identically with a program for product inspection.

On this interpretation, then, resistance to conventional appraisal programs is eminently sound. It reflects an unwillingness to treat human beings like physical objects. The needs of the organization are obviously important, but when they come into conflict with our convictions about the worth and the dignity of the human personality, one or the other must give.

Indeed, by the fact of their resistance managers are saying that the organization must yield in the face of this fundamental human value. And they are thus being more sensitive than are personnel administrators and social scientists whose business it is to be concerned with the human problems of industry!

A New Approach

If this analysis is correct, the task before us is clear. We must find a new plan—not a compromise to hide the dilemma, but a bold move to resolve the issue.

A number of writers are beginning to approach the whole subject of management from the point of view of basic social values. Peter Drucker's concept of "management by objectives"[1] offers an unusually promising framework within which we can seek a solution. Several companies, notably General Mills, Incorporated, and General Electric Company, have been exploring different methods of appraisal which rest upon assumptions consistent with Drucker's philosophy.

Responsibility on Subordinate

This approach calls on the subordinate to establish short-term performance goals *for himself.* The superior enters the process actively only *after* the subordinate has (a) done a good deal of thinking about his job, (b) made a careful assessment of his own strengths and weaknesses, and (c) formulated some specific plans to accomplish his goals. The superior's role is to help the man relate his self-appraisal, his "targets," and his plans for the ensuing period to the realities of the organization.

The first step in this process is to arrive at a clear statement of the major features of the job. Rather than a formal job description, this is a document drawn up *by the subordinate* after studying the company-approved statement. It defines the broad areas of his responsibility as they actually work out in practice. The boss and employee discuss the draft jointly and modify it as may be necessary until both of them agree that it is adequate.

Working from this statement of responsibilities, the subordinate then establishes his goals or "targets" for a period of, say, six months. These targets are *specific* actions which the man proposes to take, i.e., setting up regular staff meetings to improve communication, reorganizing the office, completing or undertaking a certain study. Thus they are explicitly stated and accompanied by a detailed account of the actions he proposes to take to reach them. This document is, in turn, discussed with the superior and modified until both are satisfied with it.

At the conclusion of the six-month period, the subordinate makes *his own* appraisal of what he has accomplished relative to the targets he had set earlier. He substantiates it with factual data wherever possible. The "interview" is an examination by superior and subordinate together of the subordinate's self-appraisal, and it culminates in a resetting of targets for the next six months.

Of course, the superior has veto power at each step of this process; in an organizational hierarchy anything else would be unacceptable. However, in practice he rarely needs to exercise it. Most subordinates tend to underestimate both their potentialities and their achievements. Moreover, subordinates normally have an understandable wish to satisfy their boss, and are quite willing to adjust their targets or appraisals if the superior feels they are unrealistic. Actually, a much more common problem is to resist the subordinates' tendency to want the boss to tell them what to write down.

Analysis vs. Appraisal

This approach to performance appraisal differs profoundly from the conventional one, for it shifts the emphasis from *appraisal* to *analysis*. This implies a more positive approach. No longer is the subordinate being examined by the superior so that his weaknesses may be determined; rather, he is examining himself, in order to define not only his weaknesses but also his strengths and potentials. The importance of this shift of emphasis should not be underestimated. It is basic to each of the specific differences which distinguish this approach from the conventional one.

The first of these differences arises from the subordinate's new role in the process. He becomes an active agent, not a passive "object." He is no longer a pawn in a chess game called management development.

Effective development of managers does not include coercing them (no matter how benevolently) into acceptance of the goals of the enterprise, nor does it mean manipulating their behavior to suit organizational needs. Rather, it calls for creating a relationship within which a man can take responsibility for developing his own potentialities, plan for himself, and learn from putting his plans into action. In the process, he can gain a genuine sense of satisfaction, for he is utilizing his own capabilities to achieve simultaneously both his objectives and those of the organization. Unless this is the nature of the relationship, "development" becomes a euphemism.

Who Knows Best?

One of the main differences of this approach is that it rests on the assumption that the individual knows—or can learn—more than anyone else about his own capabilities, needs, strengths and weaknesses, and goals. In the end, only he can determine what is best for his development. The conventional approach, on the other hand, makes the assumption that the superior can know enough about the subordinate to decide what is best for him.

No available methods can provide the superior with the knowledge he needs to make such decisions. Ratings, aptitude and personality tests, and the superior's necessarily limited knowledge of the man's performance yield at best an imperfect picture. Even the most extensive psychological counseling (assuming the superior possesses the competence for it) would not solve the problem because the product of counseling is self-insight on the part of the *counselee*.

(Psychological tests are not being condemned by this statement. On the contrary, they have genuine value in competent hands. Their use by professionals as part of the process of screening applicants for employment does not raise the same questions as their use to "diagnose" the personal worth of accepted members of a management team. Even in the latter instance, the problem under discussion would not arise if test results and interpretations were given *to the individual himself,* to be shared with superiors at his discretion.)

The proper role for the superior, then, is the one that falls naturally to him under the suggested plan: helping the subordinate relate his career planning to the needs and realities of the organization. In the discussions, the boss can use his knowledge of the organization to help the subordinate establish targets and methods for achieving them which will (a) lead to increased knowledge and skill, (b) contribute to organizational objectives, and (c) test the subordinate's appraisal of himself.

This is help which the subordinate wants. He knows well the rewards and satisfactions he seeks from his career as a manager depend on his contribution to organizational objectives. He is also aware that the superior knows more completely than he what is required for success in this organization and *under this boss.* The superior, then, is the person who can help him test the soundness of his goals and his plans for achieving them. Quite clearly the knowledge and active participation of *both* superior and subordinate are necessary components of this approach.

If the superior accepts this role, he need not become a judge of the subordinate's personal worth. He is not telling, deciding, criticizing, or praising—not "playing God." He finds himself listening, using his own knowledge of the organization as a basis for advising, guiding, encouraging his subordinates to develop their own potentialities. Incidentally, this often leads the superior to important insights about himself and his impact on others.

Looking to the Future

Another significant difference is that the emphasis is on the future rather than the past. The purpose of the plan is to establish realistic targets and to seek the most effective ways of reaching them. Appraisal thus becomes a means to a *constructive* end. The 60-year-old "coaster" can be encouraged to set performance goals for himself and to make a fair appraisal of his progress toward them. Even the subordinate who has failed can be helped to consider what moves will be best for himself. The superior rarely finds himself facing the uncomfortable prospect of denying a subordinate's personal worth. A transfer or even a demotion can be worked out without the connotation of a "sentence by the judge."

Performance vs. Personality

Finally, the accent is on *performance,* on actions relative to goals. There is less tendency for the personality of the subordinate to become an issue. The superior, instead of finding himself in the position of a psychologist or a therapist, can become a coach helping the subordinate to reach his own decisions on the specific steps that will enable him to reach his targets. Such counseling as may be required demands no deep analysis of the personal motivations or basic adjustment of the subordinate. To illustrate:

Consider a subordinate who is hostile, short-tempered, uncooperative, insecure. The superior need not make any psychological diagnosis. The "target setting" approach naturally directs the subordinate's attention to ways and means of obtaining better interdepartmental collaboration, reducing complaints, winning the confidence of the men under him. Rather than facing the troublesome prospect of forcing his own psychological diagnosis on the subordinate, the superior can, for example, help the individual plan ways of getting "feedback" concerning his impact on his associates and subordinates as a basis for self-appraisal and self-improvement.

There is little chance that a man who is involved in a process like this will be in the dark about where he stands, or that he will forget he is the principal participant in his own development and responsible for it.

A New Attitude

As a consequence of these differences we may expect the growth of a different attitude toward appraisal on the part of superior and subordinate alike.

The superior will gain real satisfaction as he learns to help his subordinates integrate so that both are served. Once the subordinate has worked out a mutually satisfactory plan of action, the superior can delegate to him the responsibility for putting it into effect. He will see himself in a consistent managerial role rather than being forced to adopt the basically incompatible role of either the judge or the psychologist.

Unless there is a basic personal antagonism between the two men (in which case the relationship should be terminated), the superior can conduct these interviews so that both are actively involved in seeking the right basis for constructive action. The organization, the boss, and the subordinate all stand to gain. Under such circumstances the opportunities for learning and for genuine development of both parties are maximal.

The particular mechanics are of secondary importance. The needs of the organization in the administration of salary and promotion policies can easily be met within the framework of the analysis process. The machinery of the program can be adjusted to the situation. No universal list of rating categories is required. The complications of subjective or prejudiced judgment, of varying standards, of attempts to quantify qualitative data, all can be minimized. In fact, no formal machinery is required.

Problems of Judgment

I have deliberately slighted the many problems of judgment involved in administering promotions and salaries. These are by no means minor, and this approach will not automatically solve them. However, I believe that if we are prepared to recognize the fundamental problem inherent in the conventional approach, ways can be found to temper our present administrative methods.

And if this approach is accepted, the traditional ingenuity of management will lead to the invention of a variety of methods for its implementation. The mechanics of some conventional plans can be adjusted to be consistent with this point of view. Obviously, a program utilizing ratings of the personal characteristics of subordinates would not be suitable, but one which emphasizes *behavior* might be.

Of course, managerial skill is required. No method will eliminate that. This method can fail as readily as any other in the clumsy hands of insensitive or indifferent or power-seeking managers. But even the limited experience of a few companies with this approach indicates that managerial *resistance* is substantially reduced. As a consequence, it is easier to gain the collaboration of managers in developing the necessary skills.

Cost in Time

There is one unavoidable cost: the manager must spend considerably more time in implementing a program of this kind. It is not unusual to take a couple of days to work through the initial establishment of responsibilities and goals with each individual. And a periodic appraisal may require several hours rather than the typical 20 minutes.

Reaction to this cost will undoubtedly vary. The management that considers the development of its human resources to be the primary means of achieving the economic objectives of the organization will not be disturbed. It will regard the necessary guidance and coaching as among the most important functions of every superior.

Conclusion

I have sought to show that the conventional approach to performance appraisal stands condemned as a personnel method. It places the manager in the untenable position of judging the personal worth of his subordinates, and of acting on these judgments. No manager possesses, nor could he acquire, the skill necessary to carry out this responsibility effectively. Few would even be willing to accept it if they were fully aware of the implications involved.

It is this unrecognized aspect of conventional appraisal programs that produces the widespread uneasiness and even open resistance of management to appraisals and especially to the appraisal interview.

A sounder approach, which places the major responsibility on the subordinate for establishing performance goals and appraising progress toward them, avoids the major weaknesses of the old plan and benefits the organization by stimulating the development of the subordinate. It is true that more managerial skill and the investment of a considerable amount of time are required, but the greater motivation and the more effective development of subordinates can justify these added costs.

If we can learn how to realize the potential for collaboration inherent in the human resources of industry, we will provide a model for governments and nations which mankind sorely needs. Douglas McGregor, *The Human Side of Enterprise* (New York, McGraw-Hill, 1960) p. 246.

[1] See *The Practice of Management* (New York, Harper & Brothers, 1954).

Index

LaVergne, TN USA
29 March 2010
177447LV00002B/1/P